Infinite Wealth Concepts

Unlocking the Financial Secrets to Building Wealth through Real Estate, Life Insurance, Brokerages, and Digital Currency

Randy Webb Jr.

All rights reserved.

No portion of this book may be reproduced in any form without written permission from the publisher or author, except as permitted by U.S. copyright law.

This publication is designed to provide accurate and authoritative information in regard to the subject matter covered. It is sold with the understanding that neither the author nor the publisher is engaged in rendering legal, investment, accounting or other professional services. While the publisher and author have used their best efforts in preparing this book, they make no representations or warranties with respect to the accuracy or completeness of the contents of this book and specifically disclaim any implied warranties of merchantability or fitness for a particular purpose. No warranty may be created or extended by sales representatives or written sales materials. The advice and strategies contained herein may not be suitable for your situation. You should consult with a professional when appropriate. Neither the publisher nor the author shall be liable for any loss of profit or any other commercial damages, including but not limited to special, incidental, consequential, personal, or other damages.

Copyright © 2023 by Randy Webb, Jr.

Life is not only about reaching your destination, but also about savoring the journey and learning from the lessons gained along the way. The wisdom gained from our experiences is a precious gift to be shared with others.

Randy Webb, Jr.

Table of Contents

INTRODUCTION	1
CHAPTER ONE: THE CREATION OF A FEDERAL MONSTER	6
FAMILY TIES	16
MEETING ON JEKYLL ISLAND	20
THE FRACTIONAL RESERVE SYSTEM	24
HOW MONEY IS CREATED ELECTRONICALLY THROUGH THE FRACTIONAL RESERVE SYSTEM	25
CHAPTER TWO: SOUND MONEY	37
SOUND MONEY	43
CHAPTER THREE: IN DEBT, WE TRUST	49
CHAPTER FOUR: THE SYSTEM	62
PROMOTE MAXIMUM EMPLOYMENT	65
PROMOTE STABLE PRICES	67
PROMOTE LONG TERM INTEREST RATES	70
INFLATION DISCRIMINATES	71
INFLATION IS MANUFACTURED	74
CHAPTER FIVE: THE 401K FUGAZI	81
HIDDEN FEES	84
THE IMPACT OF INFLATION ON YOUR RETIREMENGT PLAN	87
THE IMPACT OF TAXES ON YOUR RETIREMENT PLAN	90
THE IMPACT OF GVERNMENTL LEGISTLATION ON RETIREMENT PLANS	91
CHAPTER SIX: CREATING YOUR BANK	95
CHAPTER SEVEN: THE BLOCKCHAIN AND CRYPTOCURRENCY EXPLAINED	100
BLOCKCHAIN TECHNOLOGY EXPLAINED	101
BITCOIN EXPLAINED	105

Table of Contents

CRYPTOCURRENCY SECURITY — 106

CHAPTER EIGHT: THE POWER OF DECENTRALIZED FINANCE (DEFI). — 108

CHAPTER NINE: CREATING A PERSINAL BANKING SYSTEM WITH MAX-FUNDED AND INFINITE BANKING POLICIES — 111

CHAPTER TEN: CREATING A BANKING SYSTEM WITH YOUR BROKERAGE ACCOUNT — 115

CHAPTER ELEVEN: LEVERAGING REAL ESTATE IN A BANKING SYSTEM — 118

CHAPTER TWELVE: PURCHASING YOUR FIRST REAL ESTATE ASSET WITH 0-3.5% DOWN — 121

CONCLUSION — 127

ACKNOWLEDGEMENTS — 132

MEET THE AUTHOR — 134

Introduction

Welcome to Infinite Wealth Concepts! Fourteen years ago, I embarked on a journey to build wealth for my family and deepen my understanding of money. Throughout my journey, I realized that there were many things I didn't understand about money, along with 84% of the population. According to research conducted by the TIAA Institute on "A New Measure of Financial Literacy," only 16% of people understand the basics of money and finance.

In Infinite Wealth Concepts, we will teach the history of money and its future trajectory. This will equip you with a strategy to leverage your current financial situation and establish your banking system. In simple words, this book will guide you step-by-step on how to get out of debt by helping you fund your first Banking System in the Digital Asset Market.

There has never been a better time to enter this financial market and position yourself among the top 3% in the USA or the top 0.65% globally. The top 0.65% of the world has accumulated at least $1 million measured in US dollars. How did this small group achieve this, and is it possible for you?

Wealth is possible for anyone who starts accumulating it. However, one of the first issues we must tackle is DEBT.

Debt is taking most people by storm, and it is a blindfold for most people to move past owing money versus accumulating money. The world's debt rose by over 300 trillion dollars by the end of 2022. No one is safe! In the United States, household debt has risen by $320 billion, bringing total household debt to 17 trillion dollars as of 2023. This debt includes mortgages, auto loans, student loans, credit cards, and other debts. Most people are drowning in debt and don't know where to turn to get out of their current financial situation.

The old solution of going to the bank and begging them for a personal bailout in the form of a consolidation loan has put most people in a worse-off situation that they can't get themselves out of. The solution is twofold: first, educate people about money and then show them how to create wealth-building strategies without accumulating more debt.

Growing up, I was taught to work hard to achieve the American Dream. The American dream for most meant achieving a better and more prosperous life with no limitations or barriers. However, that has changed a lot since the

"American Dream" was introduced by author and historian James Truslow Adams in 1931. Unfortunately, the dollar's purchasing power has only moved in one direction since its inception in 1913 – downward.

In later chapters, we will go into more detail but understand that we no longer live in our grandparents and great-grandparents' economy. We must move much differently and understand how monetary policy will impact our families in the future. According to the Consumer Price Index Inflation calculator from the Bureau of Labor Statistics, 100 dollars of buying power in 1913 would equal around $3.00 today. If citizens are still following industrial age thinking, where the norm is to go to school, get good grades, and obtain a good job to retire, inflation is taking away their chances of achieving a better life and gaining wealth. Corporations are no longer required to ensure that their employees will have an actual retirement when they are of age. This has now become the employee's responsibility, who typically has limited knowledge about money and an understanding of monetary policies. Hence, this is where the problem sets in. This shift was demonstrated by General Motors, one of the largest employers in the US, when they moved from a Defined Pension Plan to a 401(K)-contribution plan in 2012. Instead of the employer providing a set amount to the employee at retirement with the defined pension plan, the burden now rests on the employee to invest their money into an investment vehicle, hoping it will perform enough to retire them in a 40-year time frame. However, what wasn't disclosed when the 401(K) contribution plans were created under the Revenue Act of 1978 was that it wasn't meant to be a primary retirement vehicle. Early adopters acknowledged that they used estimates that were too optimistic. As of 2021, almost half of the baby boomers don't have enough to retire. According to the Center on Budget and Policy Priorities, most baby boomers would be in poverty without social security. In an article by CNBC, the "father of the 401(k)," Ted Benna, stated that he regrets helping open the door for Wall Street to make more commissions than they were already making. Yes, Wall Street is getting richer off 401(k) plans more than the contributors themselves. With all the hidden fees, 401(k) recipients can expect to pay well over $100K in fees over the life of their 401(k) plan, which is not required to be disclosed.

So, where do we go from here? How do we fix this problem and give people back the power to accumulate wealth on their own? In the following chapters, we will guide you through how to start funding your bank by transferring your debt into an accumulation vehicle, allowing you to buy and borrow against your assets accumulated by "Paying Yourself First" before paying any expenses. Imagine still creating wealth on leveraged assets like Stocks, Real Estate, Life Insurance, or cryptocurrency. Congratulations on the first step toward creating your wealth accumulation vehicle that will one day allow your family to start living off the interest of your assets.

Chapter One: The Creation of a Federal Monster

"The world needs banking, but it does not need banks."
– Bill Gates

The founder of Microsoft, Bill Gates, understood something that most of the world is just now catching on to. From his statement, Bill Gates was ahead of the crisis that we would go through by relinquishing control to the banks to do our banking for us. So, what is banking? It is accepting and safeguarding money owed by other individuals and entities, then lending money to create a profit. Bill Gates was 14 years ahead of his time before a system would be created to empower and give power to the people to do their banking. However, the question that we must answer is: why should we control our own money? Is the Federal Reserve performing in our best interest?

The Federal Reserve Act mandates that its monetary policy promote maximum employment, stable prices, and moderate long-term interest rates. These mandates are all noble; however, the problem is that, after printing so much money, the economy stops responding similarly. As of this writing, the

United States national debt is at $32 trillion, inflation is through the roof, interest rates have gone from an all-time low to an all-time high, and the economy is still not responding. What does this mean? Let's break down each mandate to see how the Federal Reserve performs.

To maximize employment, the Federal Reserve lowers interest rates to promote business growth and expansion, hoping businesses will take advantage of the low loan rates and hire more employees. Unfortunately, while lowering interest rates, the Feds printed over $2.7 trillion, about 40% of the current money supply in 12 months. This brings us to the second mandate of maximizing stable prices or keeping inflation moderate. However, inflation is currently through the roof, with gas prices reaching an all-time high of $3.50 to $6.00 nationwide. Inflation is high because the Feds are trying to address two problems that require opposite solutions. To maximize employment, rates must be lowered, and rates must be raised to combat inflation. The economy is in a downward spiral, and the things that used to get an economic response to get the economy going in the right direction are no longer working. This monster was created in 1913: The Federal

Reserve, charged with establishing economic stability in the United States. However, ever since its creation and the introduction of the US dollar, the currency has only gone in one direction, and that's down. How did it all begin?

First, let's talk about how the Federal Reserve came about and gained control over the US money system. Banking is nothing new to mankind and has been around since 1800 BC. During those times, banking was done by moneylenders or financiers, who would loan and exchange money. Some of you may be familiar with how Jesus flipped the tables over in the temple of Jerusalem; guess what? Those were moneylenders and exchangers. However, when the Roman Empire collapsed, the existence of banking disappeared for a short time and didn't show up again until around the 12th and 13th centuries in Italy. In England, banks started appearing again in the 17th century. People would use goldsmiths to deposit their money to keep it safe, and in return, the goldsmiths gave them a promissory note to get their coins back on demand when requested. Depositors found that instead of using coins, it was easier to exchange promissory notes instead of coins, hence the beginning of paper money. During this time, banking was limited to people depositing money to earn interest, and those who borrowed money and paid interest on what they borrowed. Governments would borrow money during wartime from the wealthy and later pay it back plus interest through the money they got by taxing the people. One thing you'll understand as we go further into detail is that banks and money were always leveraged as a tool of war.

The timeline for banking in America started during the colonial reign of the British. Between 1690 and 1776, Americans were limited to using British money consisting of coins, commodities, and paper money. Their paper money was typically backed by land or metals, and wealthy financiers or merchants issued the extension of credit and loans. After America gained its independence after the war in 1776, it introduced central banking by ratifying the US Constitution in 1789 to solve the country's credit problems caused by the war. Alexander Hamilton, one of the Founding Fathers of The United States, set the groundwork and plan for the first Central Bank of America. Alexander Hamilton was a military commander, lawyer, banker, and economist who was a very influential interpreter of the US Constitution and is documented as the founder of the nation's financial system. He became the first Secretary of the Treasury. He implemented the first central banking system for three reasons: to provide credit to the government and businesses, establish a national currency, and handle all financial matters for the government. However, the creation of this central banking system was not without opposition. Thomas Jefferson, another Founding Father of the United States and the first Secretary of State, were suspicious about the Central bank and government that Alexander Hamilton was advocating for. Alexander H. was a Federalist who believed in big government, while Thomas Jefferson opposed this view. He believed it was an extension of the European-style monarchy that would eventually lead to massive poverty in the country due to neglect. Jefferson had a vision of farmers being able to own their land and control their destinies. Hamilton and Jefferson argued their points about their stance, ultimately leading to Hamilton winning the debate. In 1791, the First Central Bank of the United States was created, only to fail 20 years later after failing to be rechartered. Thomas Jefferson would later show his strong opposition to the Federalist party by creating the Democratic-Republican party. In 1801, Thomas

Jefferson ran for President, defeating the incumbent John Adams and ensuring that the central bank would not be rechartered.

When this central bank era ended, states began reissuing their currencies as they did when they were colonies. This lasted for a short time until President James Madison took office. The second Central Bank was chartered in 1816, lasting until 1836, when it was later declared unconstitutional and vetoed by President James Madison. As you may already realize from American history, quarrels have always existed over centralized and decentralized control. There was a 25-year period in the history of banking between 1837 to 1863 where over 8,000 state banks were created, issuing their paper notes with no regulation by the federal government. These state-chartered banks were responsible for exchanging paper notes for gold and silver. However, this would end after the nation realized it needed a much stronger monetary policy to finance the Civil War. In 1863, the National Bank Act, implemented by the North, would create a new national banking system. This system established several legislatures to fund the war: (1) establish the US Dollar as the national currency; (2) establish national banks based on a federal charter, now creating federal and state banks; (3) establish the Office of the Comptroller of the Currency to oversee national banks; (4) increase federal excise tax on state banknotes from 2 percent to 10 percent to eliminate state banknotes, hence replacing them with federal notes. As we continue, you will see some of these same behaviors happening today to crush competition entering the financial sector. After this system was created, many problems would spawn from this decentralized national banking system. There were many periods when banks would not have enough cash on hand to service customers, causing national panics with other banks, which caused a massive run on the banks. Bank runs were when depositors feared the bank would fail, so they would all rush to withdraw their money. Massive bank failures continued to happen until 1907. Eventually, they ended because of a financier named John Pierpont Morgan, who decided to use his wealth to help offer banks emergency loans. Due to the turmoil that national banks had caused, most Americans were convinced that the nation needed a central banking authority to oversee the money supply and provide a currency that could expand and contract the economy based on its needs. This is where the story begins. How was the last United States central bank formed? You may have heard that the "Federal Reserve Bank" is not a federal bank, as the name suggests, and if we can be honest, they don't carry enough reserves to be a reserve bank. So, who and what interests do they serve? In the late 1800s to early 1900s, about 25 percent of the world's wealth was held by six elite families: the Morgans, Rockefellers, Rothschilds, Warburgs, Kuhn, and Loeb. These families would create a legacy in our history of money and banking that would be a staple forever. In almost everything we do today, these six elite names are intertwined. Each of them stamped their name in the history of investing and banking. If you don't understand anything you read over the next couple of paragraphs, I want you to take away that banking is everyone's business, no matter what they do. Before elaborating on the secret meeting on Jekyll Island off the coast of Georgia to form the Federal Reserve, you must first understand the family lineage.

    The Rothschild family dynasty is one of the most prominent banking families in the world. They rose to power through Mayer Amschel Rothschild, a Jewish banker who handled the finances of European and German royalty during the late 1700s to early 1800s. Through his services to the Holy Roman Empire, he gained noble status in both the Holy Roman Empire and the United Kingdom. He was thoughtful about keeping wealth within the family, and he had five sons who would carry on the international banking dynasty. He sent them to London, Paris, Frankfurt, Vienna, and Naples to start their banks. Mayer Rothschild is also known for making the famous statement about the money supply: "I care not what puppet is placed upon the throne of England to rule the Empire on which the sun never sets. The man who controls the British money supply controls the British Empire, and I control the British money supply." He did precisely as he preached, and they stayed in control of their family's banking system, rising to have the most considerable private fortune in the world. Today, the Rothschild family owns a 37% stake in the Rockefeller Wealth Management group in the United States.

  The next significant name in the banking industry is John Pierpont Morgan, also known as J.P. Morgan. He was a financier and banker who gained a lot of footing on Wall Street. He bailed out the national banking industry in the early 1900s, which later gave him an in to create the most powerful central bank that would ever exist, "The Fed." He was the head of the banking firm that became JP Morgan & Company, where he accumulated wealth in major industries and companies still in business today. As a banker, he had interests in the US steel industry, agriculture, automobiles, construction, commercial trucks, lawn and garden products, and household goods. His hands were in almost everything, and he also had controlling interest in companies like Aetna, Western Union, Pullman Car Company, 21 railroads, and General Electric. Today, you may have seen his name on one of the largest ranked banks in the United States, JPMorgan Chase Bank, with a total asset worth over $3 billion.

Abraham Kuhn and his brother-in-law Solomon Loeb were among the other elite names that would be staples in American history. The two started an investment bank in 1867 called Kuhn, Loeb & Co. In 1865, they started manufacturing men's clothing and made a fortune supplying uniforms for the military before deciding to enter the investment banking industry. Their names still live on through companies like the "Lehman Brothers" and "American Express."

John D. Rockefeller, who has been stated to be one of the wealthiest Americans of all time, is considered one of the elite family names in America. Rockefeller was an American business owner who started one of the world's first and most significant oil companies through "The Standard Oil Company." At one point in US History, John Rockefeller had a 90 percent controlling interest in ALL oil in the United States. His wealth peaked as kerosene and gasoline became very important with the invention of electricity and automobiles. He revolutionized the petroleum industry and is known to be one of the first billionaires of his time. However, due to antitrust laws, also known as monopoly laws, he divided his company into 34 separate entities to avoid this law.

Family Ties:

When I started writing this book, I didn't know what I would uncover regarding family ties. I found that each of these elite families who gained control over the United States' financial system kept the wealth close to the family. It would only be right to walk you through how the families tied together before the meeting on Jekyll Island. In 1916, Forbes released an article highlighting seven men of influence who met on Jekyll Island for a secret meeting to roll out a reform to form the Federal Reserve. Nelson W. Aldrich, who was the leader of the Republican Party in the United States Senate; Abram Piatt Andrew, an Assistant Professor of Economics at Harvard University, Assistant Secretary of the Treasury, and a member of the US House of Representatives; Henry Pomeroy Davison Sr., a banker and senior partner at JP Morgan & Company in 1909; Frank A. Vanderlip Sr., who was a banker, President of the National City Bank of New York, now known as Citibank, and Assistant Secretary of Treasury; Arthur Shelton, the Private Secretary to Senator Aldrich; Paul Moritz Warsburg, an investment banker, the Director of Wells Fargo, and a significant advocate for implementing the US Central banking system; and lastly, Benjamin Strong Jr., another banker, Vice President of Bankers Trust, later becoming the President and also ended up serving as the Governor of the Federal Reserve.

 Of these seven men, there were close relationship ties that would keep the lineage of these elites in power. What all these men have in common is their connection to John P. Morgan. After researching the family lineage of J.P. Morgan

Sr., we find that J.P. Morgan Jr. and John D. Rockefeller, two of the wealthiest men of their time, were 7th cousins leading up to their great-grandparents, James Morgan & Margery Hill, who had two sons, James Morgan who would be the ascendant of John D. Rockefeller, and Joseph Morgan who would be the ascendant of J.P. Morgan Jr. Senator Nelson Aldrich's fourth child, Abigail Nelson, married John D. Rockefeller Jr., who was the only son of John D. Rockefeller Sr. John D. Rockefeller Jr. & Abigail Aldrich Rockefeller would birth six children, and three would go off to become politicians; Nelson A. Rockefeller, 49th Governor of New York and 41st Vice President of America; Winthrop Rockefeller, 37th Governor of Arkansas; and David Rockefeller, Chairman of the Council of Foreign Affairs and CEO of Chase National Bank.

    Abram P. Andrew was the Director of the US Mint from 1909-1910 and the Assistant Secretary of the Treasury from 1910 to 1912, when Senator Nelson Aldrich was the Republican Majority leader of the Senate. Henry P. Davison Sr. was connected to J.P. Morgan Sr. because he worked for his firm as a partner. Frank A. Vanderlip served as the Assistant Secretary of the Treasury from 1897 to 1901, which connected him to Senator Nelson Aldrich. He also worked closely with J.P Morgan Sr. during the bank panic in 1907. Most of J.P. Morgan's influence happened during the panic in 1907, as he was considered the savior of the banking industry. Arthur Shelton was the private secretary to Senator Aldrich and was also placed on the board for the private meeting in Jekyll Island. Lastly, Paul Warburg, who married Nina Loeb, the daughter of Solomon Loeb, the founder of Kuhn, Loeb & Co Investment bank, placed the Kuhn-Loeb family at the table. Paul Warburg also had a direct connection to J.P. Morgan as he was the Chairman of J.P. Morgan & Co. Benjamin Strong, another member at the Jekyll Island secret meeting, had a connection with J.P. Morgan as he worked for the second-largest US Trust company that was dominant on Wall Street. Three of J.P. Morgan & Co. associates held the voting power of this company, which caused him to work closely with J.P. Morgan during the bank panic in 1907. Through these close ties, all six elite family names had some representation at the meeting off the coast of Georgia on Jekyll Island.

Meeting on Jekyll Island

Over the past century, the concept of central banking has sparked many debates among politicians on whether there should be a centralized or decentralized authority. After the last bank run with a semi-central bank in place, the people were ready to put something in place to unify the national banking system that was currently in place. J.P. Morgan, in 1907, was credited with ending the banking panic by using his wealth to rescue the banking system. This gave him significant influence in the early 1900s, and there is no doubt that he had a lot of influence over the financial system that would be created.

The secret meeting on Jekyll Island is no longer a secret, as there have been many articles and books written about how this meeting would influence the banking system in the world. In November of 1910, Senator Nelson Aldrich arranged a secret meeting on Jekyll Island off the coast of Georgia under the guise of a hunting trip. The Jekyll Island Club was an exclusive club to which J.P. Morgan belonged. Although Morgan was not physically present, it was said that he arranged the meeting at the club. The men who attended the meeting on Jekyll Island were all selected to serve in a study group called the National

Monetary Commission, created by the Aldrich-Vreeland Act of 1908 after the bank panic of 1907. The meeting was so secretive that the men used only their first names to avoid drawing attention to themselves on the way to Jekyll Island. The group was assembled to study banking laws in the United States and Europe. The National Monetary Commission consisted of 18 members, but only seven were invited to Jekyll Island to formulate the Central Bank for the United States.

    According to multiple sources, the meeting was kept secret because politicians and bankers did not believe the public would be receptive to proposals for a Central Bank created by bankers on Wall Street. Did the public have a good reason not to trust this committee? Let's look at what came out of the meeting. Aldrich's proposal was criticized by the Senate and Congress, as they believed that the National Reserve Association proposal gave too little control to the government and too much power to the bankers, especially those who ran large organizations. Therefore, most people believe that JP Morgan influenced the bill to serve him and Wall Street. Aldrich's proposal created a 46-member board that would have only six members appointed by the government. This time, the government would have no stake in the Central Bank, unlike the first central banks that were attempted previously.

When this proposal was being presented, a political transition was happening that put the bankers on edge, as they did not know the destiny of the new Aldrich proposal after Democrats took control of the House and the Presidency. In 1912, President Woodrow Wilson was elected to office, and the House Banking and Currency Committee was assigned a new subcommittee to look further into the reform proposal. However, the head of the House Banking and Currency Committee, Representative Carter Glass, ended up with similar ideals to the proposal that Aldrich presented, except that he believed regional banks should be autonomous and have limited governmental control. Glass's proposal also gave complete authority to the bankers. President Wilson, however, knew that neither Congress nor the public would accept a central banking system with no government control. Therefore, he added a provision that created an oversight board called the "Federal Reserve Board," with members appointed by the President who previously held government positions.

The Federal Reserve Banking System was established in 1913 through the Federal Reserve Act, creating the most robust Central Bank in the world with twelve regional reserve banks nationwide. This Central Banking system controlled all banking activities and enforced a monetary policy to promote maximum employment, stable prices, and moderate long-term interest rates. The Federal Reserve was given full authority and power to print money, adjust interest rates, and buy and sell US Treasuries to achieve this. Today, the Federal Reserve uses quantitative easing to stimulate the economy, which includes printing "Fiat" money to purchase Treasury securities and inject new money into the economy.

"Fiat" money has no intrinsic value except that it has been declared legal tender by the government. The Federal Reserve purchases government debt with "Fiat" money, then uses the debt they purchased as reserves to create more "Fiat" money to lend to the public. In this process, money is not created until it is borrowed. Therefore, the Federal Reserve Bank needs people to stay in debt to create an endless money supply. The more money people borrow, the more money the government can create; the more people borrow, the more they must work.

Ultimately, this creates a situation where people work to pay off government debt that can never be paid off to support their basic needs.

The Fractional Reserve System

The Federal Reserve system operates on a fractional reserve banking system, allowing banks to keep a small portion of cash on hand to cover a fraction of the bank deposits. This system is used to free up capital for lending. If everyone who deposited money into the bank showed up to withdraw their money, the bank would not be able to give everyone their money. The Federal Reserve sets the banks' reserves, typically 10 percent. For example, if someone deposited $100 into their bank account, the bank could loan out $90 and keep $10 as reserves. As mentioned earlier, the US dollar is backed by government debt, and money is not created until borrowed. Therefore, since the dollar is a debt instrument, the Federal Reserve pays the banks interest for their reserve balance. The Federal Reserve uses this tool to implement monetary policy. If they increase reserve requirements, it decreases the credit that banks can extend to the public, ultimately restraining economic activities. If they decrease reserve requirements, it allows banks to lend out more money to stimulate the economy. In March 2020, during the kickoff of the COVID pandemic, the Federal Reserve announced no reserve requirements for depository institutions. This means a bank does not have to keep any cash reserves. They can loan out 100 percent of your money once you deposit it to create more money.

How Money is Created Electronically Through the Fractional Reserve System

Let's explore how banks create money by lending out funds using their reserves. Remember, if they keep a reserve on hand, the Federal Reserve pays them interest on the reserves they hold in physical cash. You may wonder why the banks are getting paid an interest rate for holding your deposits as a reserve. It's simple! They are holding onto government debt as reserves. The US dollar is a debt instrument backed by governmental debt. For the Federal Reserve to insert new money into the economy for banks to loan out for public consumption, they must first print money and then buy US Treasury bonds, which are "government debt," and then place these U.S. Treasury bonds on their balance sheet as reserves. So, the banks get paid interest because they are holding physical debt instruments known as Federal Reserve Notes, aka the U.S. dollar, issued by the Federal Reserve.

The Federal Reserve understands that new money injected into the economy is not considered real money until consumers borrow it. This is because the U.S. dollar is a fiat currency that is not backed by anything except the government debt behind it. When consumers borrow money from banks, they are charged interest rates, which is how money is created. Lowering interest rates is one way the Federal Reserve entices consumers to borrow more money. The year 2021 saw record-low home loan interest rates of 1.75 percent, while the government printed trillions of dollars. However, the situation changed significantly towards the end of 2022 and in 2023, interest rates reached an all-time high, and inflation remained uncontrolled. Despite this, there was a surge in demand for homes, which led to sellers raising their prices above the usual rate. Additionally, inflation resulted in an increase in the value of material goods due to the decreased value of the dollar. Currently, the US national debt is at $32 trillion, and the

Federal Reserve prints about 40 million physical notes daily with a total face value of $430 billion annually. This excludes electronic money created through the fractional reserve system or already in circulation. Figure 1 illustrates how electronic money is created through the fractional reserve system, assuming an average 10 percent reserve requirement. The example shows that the initial $1,000 deposit can create an additional $9,000 without the Federal Reserve printing any physical currency. However, as of March 26, 2020, the Federal Reserve removed all reserve requirements to meet its monetary policy. Figure 2 shows what happens when $1,000 is deposited with no reserve requirements, resulting in an infinite multiplication of funds. Finally, we will provide a real-life example of the money generated with the current print order and monetary policy.

The Board of Governors of the Federal Reserve System has announced that they expect to print 9.6 billion notes valued at $430 billion for the fiscal year, a 65% increase from the previous year. Figure 3 demonstrates that an injection of $430 billion into the economy with a 10% reserve requirement would generate $4.3 trillion through the fractional reserve system after

73 cycles. Figure 4 illustrates what $430 billion generates with no reserves after 73 cycles, with infinite cycles possible without reserve requirements. The injection of more fiat currency into the economy leads to increased costs of goods, which reduces the buying power of the working class. This system creates an enslaved environment where people must work to satisfy their basic needs. Due to uncontrollable inflation, CNBC has reported that full-time minimum-wage workers can no longer afford rent anywhere in the United States. Printing money that causes inflation is essentially a hidden tax on the people. The current economy is vastly different from that of previous generations.

Example on how a $1,000 deposit creates an additional $9,000 in electronic money through the Fractional Reserve System

Bank	Initial Deposit	Reserves	Loan
1	$ 1,000.00	$ 100.00	$ 900.00
2	$ 900.00	$ 90.00	$ 810.00
3	$ 810.00	$ 81.00	$ 729.00
4	$ 729.00	$ 72.90	$ 656.10
5	$ 656.10	$ 65.61	$ 590.49
6	$ 590.49	$ 59.05	$ 531.44
7	$ 531.44	$ 53.14	$ 478.30
8	$ 478.30	$ 47.83	$ 430.47
9	$ 430.47	$ 43.05	$ 387.42
10	$ 387.42	$ 38.74	$ 348.68
11	$ 348.68	$ 34.87	$ 313.81
12	$ 313.81	$ 31.38	$ 282.43
13	$ 282.43	$ 28.24	$ 254.19
14	$ 254.19	$ 25.42	$ 228.77
15	$ 228.77	$ 22.88	$ 205.89
16	$ 205.89	$ 20.59	$ 185.30
17	$ 185.30	$ 18.53	$ 166.77
18	$ 166.77	$ 16.68	$ 150.09
19	$ 150.09	$ 15.01	$ 135.09
20	$ 135.09	$ 13.51	$ 121.58
21	$ 121.58	$ 12.16	$ 109.42
22	$ 109.42	$ 10.94	$ 98.48
23	$ 98.48	$ 9.85	$ 88.63
24	$ 88.63	$ 8.86	$ 79.77
25	$ 79.77	$ 7.98	$ 71.79
26	$ 71.79	$ 7.18	$ 64.61
27	$ 64.61	$ 6.46	$ 58.15
28	$ 58.15	$ 5.81	$ 52.33
29	$ 52.33	$ 5.23	$ 47.10
30	$ 47.10	$ 4.71	$ 42.39
31	$ 42.39	$ 4.24	$ 38.15
32	$ 38.15	$ 3.82	$ 34.34
33	$ 34.34	$ 3.43	$ 30.90
34	$ 30.90	$ 3.09	$ 27.81
35	$ 27.81	$ 2.78	$ 25.03
36	$ 25.03	$ 2.50	$ 22.53
37	$ 22.53	$ 2.25	$ 20.28
38	$ 20.28	$ 2.03	$ 18.25
39	$ 18.25	$ 1.82	$ 16.42
40	$ 16.42	$ 1.64	$ 14.78
41	$ 14.78	$ 1.48	$ 13.30
42	$ 13.30	$ 1.33	$ 11.97
43	$ 11.97	$ 1.20	$ 10.78
44	$ 10.78	$ 1.08	$ 9.70
45	$ 9.70	$ 0.97	$ 8.73
46	$ 8.73	$ 0.87	$ 7.86

Figure 1

Example on how a $1,000 deposit creates an additional $9,000 in electronic money through the Fractional Reserve System

47	$ 7.86	$ 0.79	$ 7.07
48	$ 7.07	$ 0.71	$ 6.36
49	$ 6.36	$ 0.64	$ 5.73
50	$ 5.73	$ 0.57	$ 5.15
51	$ 5.15	$ 0.52	$ 4.64
52	$ 4.64	$ 0.46	$ 4.17
53	$ 4.17	$ 0.42	$ 3.76
54	$ 3.76	$ 0.38	$ 3.38
55	$ 3.38	$ 0.34	$ 3.04
56	$ 3.04	$ 0.30	$ 2.74
57	$ 2.74	$ 0.27	$ 2.47
58	$ 2.47	$ 0.25	$ 2.22
59	$ 2.22	$ 0.22	$ 2.00
60	$ 2.00	$ 0.20	$ 1.80
61	$ 1.80	$ 0.18	$ 1.62
62	$ 1.62	$ 0.16	$ 1.46
63	$ 1.46	$ 0.15	$ 1.31
64	$ 1.31	$ 0.13	$ 1.18
65	$ 1.18	$ 0.12	$ 1.06
66	$ 1.06	$ 0.11	$ 0.96
67	$ 0.96	$ 0.10	$ 0.86
68	$ 0.86	$ 0.09	$ 0.77
69	$ 0.77	$ 0.08	$ 0.70
70	$ 0.70	$ 0.07	$ 0.63
71	$ 0.63	$ 0.06	$ 0.56
72	$ 0.56	$ 0.06	$ 0.51
73	$ 0.51	$ 0.05	$ 0.46

Total $9,995.4 $999.5 $8,995.9

Note: With just ONE initial deposit of $1,000 there was $9,000 magically created in the banking system just through the depositing of checks created by the previous bank. This illustration shows when the scheme would run out using a 10 percent reserve requirement. After about 73 deposits the $1,000 initial deposit used as reserves runs it course.

Example on how a $1,000 deposit creates an additional $73,000 in electronic money through the Fractional Reserve System. (We stopped at 73 levels but this can go infinitely)

Bank	Reserves	Loan
1	$ -	$ 1,000.00
2	$ -	$ 1,000.00
3	$ -	$ 1,000.00
4	$ -	$ 1,000.00
5	$ -	$ 1,000.00
6	$ -	$ 1,000.00
7	$ -	$ 1,000.00
8	$ -	$ 1,000.00
9	$ -	$ 1,000.00
10	$ -	$ 1,000.00
11	$ -	$ 1,000.00
12	$ -	$ 1,000.00
13	$ -	$ 1,000.00
14	$ -	$ 1,000.00
15	$ -	$ 1,000.00
16	$ -	$ 1,000.00
17	$ -	$ 1,000.00
18	$ -	$ 1,000.00
19	$ -	$ 1,000.00
20	$ -	$ 1,000.00
21	$ -	$ 1,000.00
22	$ -	$ 1,000.00
23	$ -	$ 1,000.00
24	$ -	$ 1,000.00
25	$ -	$ 1,000.00
26	$ -	$ 1,000.00
27	$ -	$ 1,000.00
28	$ -	$ 1,000.00
29	$ -	$ 1,000.00
30	$ -	$ 1,000.00
31	$ -	$ 1,000.00
32	$ -	$ 1,000.00
33	$ -	$ 1,000.00
34	$ -	$ 1,000.00
35	$ -	$ 1,000.00
36	$ -	$ 1,000.00
37	$ -	$ 1,000.00
38	$ -	$ 1,000.00
39	$ -	$ 1,000.00
40	$ -	$ 1,000.00
41	$ -	$ 1,000.00
42	$ -	$ 1,000.00
43	$ -	$ 1,000.00
44	$ -	$ 1,000.00
45	$ -	$ 1,000.00
46	$ -	$ 1,000.00

Figure 2

Example on how a $1,000 deposit creates an additional $73,000 in electronic money through the Fractional Reserve System. (We stopped at 73 levels but this can go infinitely)

47	$ -	$	1,000.00
48	$ -	$	1,000.00
49	$ -	$	1,000.00
50	$ -	$	1,000.00
51	$ -	$	1,000.00
52	$ -	$	1,000.00
53	$ -	$	1,000.00
54	$ -	$	1,000.00
55	$ -	$	1,000.00
56	$ -	$	1,000.00
57	$ -	$	1,000.00
58	$ -	$	1,000.00
59	$ -	$	1,000.00
60	$ -	$	1,000.00
61	$ -	$	1,000.00
62	$ -	$	1,000.00
63	$ -	$	1,000.00
64	$ -	$	1,000.00
65	$ -	$	1,000.00
66	$ -	$	1,000.00
67	$ -	$	1,000.00
68	$ -	$	1,000.00
69	$ -	$	1,000.00
70	$ -	$	1,000.00
71	$ -	$	1,000.00
72	$ -	$	1,000.00
73	$ -	$	1,000.00
	$ -	$	73,000.00

NOTE: This initial $1,000 deposit will go infinitely as each customer deposit their loan in to the bank. Since there are no reserve requirments the money will never stop replicating.

Figure 2

Example on how a $430 billion deposit creates an additional $4.3 Trillion in electronic money through the Fractional Reserve System

Bank	Initial Deposit	Reserves	Loan
1	$430,931,200.00	$43,093,120.00	$387,838,080.00
2	$387,838,080.00	$38,783,808.00	$349,054,272.00
3	$349,054,272.00	$34,905,427.20	$314,148,844.80
4	$314,148,844.80	$31,414,884.48	$282,733,960.32
5	$282,733,960.32	$28,273,396.03	$254,460,564.29
6	$254,460,564.29	$25,446,056.43	$229,014,507.86
7	$229,014,507.86	$22,901,450.79	$206,113,057.07
8	$206,113,057.07	$20,611,305.71	$185,501,751.37
9	$185,501,751.37	$18,550,175.14	$166,951,576.23
10	$166,951,576.23	$16,695,157.62	$150,256,418.61
11	$150,256,418.61	$15,025,641.86	$135,230,776.75
12	$135,230,776.75	$13,523,077.67	$121,707,699.07
13	$121,707,699.07	$12,170,769.91	$109,536,929.16
14	$109,536,929.16	$10,953,692.92	$98,583,236.25
15	$98,583,236.25	$9,858,323.62	$88,724,912.62
16	$88,724,912.62	$8,872,491.26	$79,852,421.36
17	$79,852,421.36	$7,985,242.14	$71,867,179.22
18	$71,867,179.22	$7,186,717.92	$64,680,461.30
19	$64,680,461.30	$6,468,046.13	$58,212,415.17
20	$58,212,415.17	$5,821,241.52	$52,391,173.65
21	$52,391,173.65	$5,239,117.37	$47,152,056.29
22	$47,152,056.29	$4,715,205.63	$42,436,850.66
23	$42,436,850.66	$4,243,685.07	$38,193,165.59
24	$38,193,165.59	$3,819,316.56	$34,373,849.03
25	$34,373,849.03	$3,437,384.90	$30,936,464.13
26	$30,936,464.13	$3,093,646.41	$27,842,817.72
27	$27,842,817.72	$2,784,281.77	$25,058,535.95
28	$25,058,535.95	$2,505,853.59	$22,552,682.35
29	$22,552,682.35	$2,255,268.24	$20,297,414.12
30	$20,297,414.12	$2,029,741.41	$18,267,672.70
31	$18,267,672.70	$1,826,767.27	$16,440,905.43
32	$16,440,905.43	$1,644,090.54	$14,796,814.89
33	$14,796,814.89	$1,479,681.49	$13,317,133.40
34	$13,317,133.40	$1,331,713.34	$11,985,420.06
35	$11,985,420.06	$1,198,542.01	$10,786,878.06
36	$10,786,878.06	$1,078,687.81	$9,708,190.25
37	$9,708,190.25	$970,819.02	$8,737,371.22
38	$8,737,371.22	$873,737.12	$7,863,634.10
39	$7,863,634.10	$786,363.41	$7,077,270.69
40	$7,077,270.69	$707,727.07	$6,369,543.62
41	$6,369,543.62	$636,954.36	$5,732,589.26
42	$5,732,589.26	$573,258.93	$5,159,330.33
43	$5,159,330.33	$515,933.03	$4,643,397.30
44	$4,643,397.30	$464,339.73	$4,179,057.57
45	$4,179,057.57	$417,905.76	$3,761,151.81
46	$3,761,151.81	$376,115.18	$3,385,036.63

Figure 3

Example on how a $430 billion deposit creates an additional $4.3 Trillion in electronic money through the Fractional Reserve System

47	$	3,385,036.63	$	338,503.66	$	3,046,532.97
48	$	3,046,532.97	$	304,653.30	$	2,741,879.67
49	$	2,741,879.67	$	274,187.97	$	2,467,691.71
50	$	2,467,691.71	$	246,769.17	$	2,220,922.53
51	$	2,220,922.53	$	222,092.25	$	1,998,830.28
52	$	1,998,830.28	$	199,883.03	$	1,798,947.25
53	$	1,798,947.25	$	179,894.73	$	1,619,052.53
54	$	1,619,052.53	$	161,905.25	$	1,457,147.27
55	$	1,457,147.27	$	145,714.73	$	1,311,432.55
56	$	1,311,432.55	$	131,143.25	$	1,180,289.29
57	$	1,180,289.29	$	118,028.93	$	1,062,260.36
58	$	1,062,260.36	$	106,226.04	$	956,034.33
59	$	956,034.33	$	95,603.43	$	860,430.89
60	$	860,430.89	$	86,043.09	$	774,387.80
61	$	774,387.80	$	77,438.78	$	696,949.02
62	$	696,949.02	$	69,694.90	$	627,254.12
63	$	627,254.12	$	62,725.41	$	564,528.71
64	$	564,528.71	$	56,452.87	$	508,075.84
65	$	508,075.84	$	50,807.58	$	457,268.25
66	$	457,268.25	$	45,726.83	$	411,541.43
67	$	411,541.43	$	41,154.14	$	370,387.29
68	$	370,387.29	$	37,038.73	$	333,348.56
69	$	333,348.56	$	33,334.86	$	300,013.70
70	$	300,013.70	$	30,001.37	$	270,012.33
71	$	270,012.33	$	27,001.23	$	243,011.10
72	$	243,011.10	$	24,301.11	$	218,709.99
73	$	218,709.99	$	21,871.00	$	196,838.99
Total		$4,307,343,610.1		$430,734,361.0		$3,876,609,249.1

Note: With just ONE initial deposit of $1,000 there was $9,000 magically created in the banking system just through the depositing of checks created by the previous bank. This illustration shows when the scheme would run out using a 10 percent reserve requirement. After about 73 deposits the $1,000 initial deposit used as reserves runs it course.

Figure 3

Example on how can $430 billion creates an inifinite amount of electronic money through the Fractional Reserve System

Bank	Initial Deposit	Reserves	Loan
1	$ 430,931,200.00	$ -	$ 430,931,200.00
2	$ 430,931,200.00	$ -	$ 430,931,200.00
3	$ 430,931,200.00	$ -	$ 430,931,200.00
4	$ 430,931,200.00	$ -	$ 430,931,200.00
5	$ 430,931,200.00	$ -	$ 430,931,200.00
6	$ 430,931,200.00	$ -	$ 430,931,200.00
7	$ 430,931,200.00	$ -	$ 430,931,200.00
8	$ 430,931,200.00	$ -	$ 430,931,200.00
9	$ 430,931,200.00	$ -	$ 430,931,200.00
10	$ 430,931,200.00	$ -	$ 430,931,200.00
11	$ 430,931,200.00	$ -	$ 430,931,200.00
12	$ 430,931,200.00	$ -	$ 430,931,200.00
13	$ 430,931,200.00	$ -	$ 430,931,200.00
14	$ 430,931,200.00	$ -	$ 430,931,200.00
15	$ 430,931,200.00	$ -	$ 430,931,200.00
16	$ 430,931,200.00	$ -	$ 430,931,200.00
17	$ 430,931,200.00	$ -	$ 430,931,200.00
18	$ 430,931,200.00	$ -	$ 430,931,200.00
19	$ 430,931,200.00	$ -	$ 430,931,200.00
20	$ 430,931,200.00	$ -	$ 430,931,200.00
21	$ 430,931,200.00	$ -	$ 430,931,200.00
22	$ 430,931,200.00	$ -	$ 430,931,200.00
23	$ 430,931,200.00	$ -	$ 430,931,200.00
24	$ 430,931,200.00	$ -	$ 430,931,200.00
25	$ 430,931,200.00	$ -	$ 430,931,200.00
26	$ 430,931,200.00	$ -	$ 430,931,200.00
27	$ 430,931,200.00	$ -	$ 430,931,200.00
28	$ 430,931,200.00	$ -	$ 430,931,200.00
29	$ 430,931,200.00	$ -	$ 430,931,200.00
30	$ 430,931,200.00	$ -	$ 430,931,200.00
31	$ 430,931,200.00	$ -	$ 430,931,200.00
32	$ 430,931,200.00	$ -	$ 430,931,200.00
33	$ 430,931,200.00	$ -	$ 430,931,200.00
34	$ 430,931,200.00	$ -	$ 430,931,200.00
35	$ 430,931,200.00	$ -	$ 430,931,200.00
36	$ 430,931,200.00	$ -	$ 430,931,200.00
37	$ 430,931,200.00	$ -	$ 430,931,200.00
38	$ 430,931,200.00	$ -	$ 430,931,200.00
39	$ 430,931,200.00	$ -	$ 430,931,200.00
40	$ 430,931,200.00	$ -	$ 430,931,200.00
41	$ 430,931,200.00	$ -	$ 430,931,200.00
42	$ 430,931,200.00	$ -	$ 430,931,200.00
43	$ 430,931,200.00	$ -	$ 430,931,200.00
44	$ 430,931,200.00	$ -	$ 430,931,200.00
45	$ 430,931,200.00	$ -	$ 430,931,200.00

Figure 4

Example on how can $430 billion creates an inifinite amount of electronic money through the Fractional Reserve System

46	$	430,931,200.00	$	-	$	430,931,200.00
47	$	430,931,200.00	$	-	$	430,931,200.00
48	$	430,931,200.00	$	-	$	430,931,200.00
49	$	430,931,200.00	$	-	$	430,931,200.00
50	$	430,931,200.00	$	-	$	430,931,200.00
51	$	430,931,200.00	$	-	$	430,931,200.00
52	$	430,931,200.00	$	-	$	430,931,200.00
53	$	430,931,200.00	$	-	$	430,931,200.00
54	$	430,931,200.00	$	-	$	430,931,200.00
55	$	430,931,200.00	$	-	$	430,931,200.00
56	$	430,931,200.00	$	-	$	430,931,200.00
57	$	430,931,200.00	$	-	$	430,931,200.00
58	$	430,931,200.00	$	-	$	430,931,200.00
59	$	430,931,200.00	$	-	$	430,931,200.00
60	$	430,931,200.00	$	-	$	430,931,200.00
61	$	430,931,200.00	$	-	$	430,931,200.00
62	$	430,931,200.00	$	-	$	430,931,200.00
63	$	430,931,200.00	$	-	$	430,931,200.00
64	$	430,931,200.00	$	-	$	430,931,200.00
65	$	430,931,200.00	$	-	$	430,931,200.00
66	$	430,931,200.00	$	-	$	430,931,200.00
67	$	430,931,200.00	$	-	$	430,931,200.00
68	$	430,931,200.00	$	-	$	430,931,200.00
69	$	430,931,200.00	$	-	$	430,931,200.00
70	$	430,931,200.00	$	-	$	430,931,200.00
71	$	430,931,200.00	$	-	$	430,931,200.00
72	$	430,931,200.00	$	-	$	430,931,200.00
73	$	430,931,200.00	$	-	$	430,931,200.00
	$	31,457,977,600.00	$	-	$	31,457,977,600.00

NOTE: The Federal Reserve print order for FY2021 is $430.9 billion which will create trillions of dollars through he fractional reserve system. In this example just going through 73 cycles or banks it created $31.4 trillion dollars.

Figure 4

Chapter Two: Sound Money

"The issuing power of money should be taken from the banks and restored to the people, to whom it properly belongs."
– Thomas Jefferson

Money, money, money...what is it? Is there a difference between types of money? What distinguishes fiat money from real or sound money? Money is defined as anything used to pay for goods and services; based on this definition, it can be anything that people are willing to accept as payment. Over 8,000 years ago, bartering was the form of payment used to exchange goods and services, but it had limitations. It was complicated to exchange goods, especially when a party did not have what the other party needed. Throughout history, many things have been used as money or a medium of exchange to buy the things people wanted. For example, Cowrie shells were used as money in China, India, and Africa in 1200 BC, but they had a divisibility problem as they could not be measured or divided.

Since the creation of the Federal Reserve Central Bank and the adoption of the US dollar, its buying power has only decreased and has not had the same value since 19 13. One hundred dollars in 1913 equals a little over $3 today, meaning the US dollar has lost 97 percent of its value since its inception. So why do people continue to work for it? The answer is that they do not fully comprehend how the current monetary system affects their family's finances in the long term. Due to the immense impact of inflation caused by monetary policy, a significant amount of wealth has been taken from people without the need for taxation.

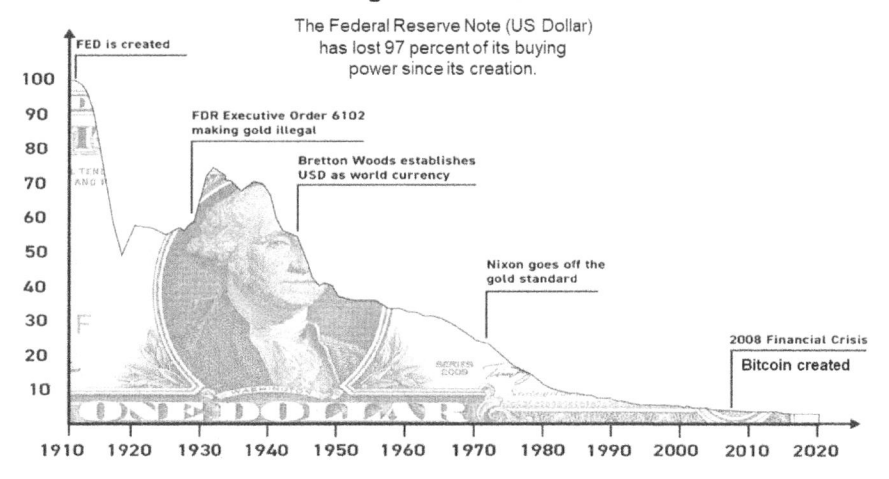

Purchasing Power of U.S. Dollar

The Federal Reserve Note (US Dollar) has lost 97 percent of its buying power since its creation.

- FED is created
- FDR Executive Order 6102 making gold illegal
- Bretton Woods establishes USD as world currency
- Nixon goes off the gold standard
- 2008 Financial Crisis
- Bitcoin created

From 1913 to 1923, the dollar's buying power decreased from 100% to 57% in just ten years. This caused a decline in confidence among the people, leading them to hoard gold to combat the dollar's depreciation. However, from 1923 to 1933, there was a slight increase in buying power, with the dollar returning to 76 percent. Unfortunately, after the 1933 Wall Street crash, the dollar's buying power never returned to its previous level. The United States had been on the gold standard since 1879, meaning each bank-issued dollar was backed by gold. However, the country lost too many gold reserves during World War I and the Great Depression of the 1930s, which hurt the economy. In March 1933, President Franklin D. Roosevelt declared a nationwide bank moratorium to prevent a run on the banks. On March 6, 1933, he issued Proclamation 2039, which suspended all banking activities immediately. According to Proclamation 2039:

"No such banking institution or branch shall pay out, export, earmark, or permit the withdrawal or transfer in any manner or by any device whatsoever of any gold or silver coin or bullion or currency, or take any other action which might facilitate the hoarding thereof, nor shall any such banking institution or branch pay out deposits, make loans or discounts, deal in foreign exchange, transfer credits from the United States to any

place abroad, or transact any other banking business whatsoever."

All banking operations were shut down for an entire week due to the bank failures and other events. In the early 1900s, banks were required to hold 40 percent of gold in ratio to the money they were issuing. However, their reserves were depleting as the world lost faith in the dollar, causing countries to redeem dollars for gold and impacting the money supply. In response, President Roosevelt issued Proclamation 2039 to allow the banks to regroup. The Emergency Banking Act was signed into legislation on March 9, 1933, to restore public confidence in the banking system. President Roosevelt stated during his address to the nation, *"I can assure you that it is safer to keep your money in a reopened bank than under the mattress."* However, citizens didn't realize that this would be the first step toward pulling the US off the gold standard, as the Emergency Act of 1933 gave the Federal Reserve the authority to issue "Federal Reserve Bank Notes" backed by any asset of the commercial bank. They no longer had to issue certificates backed by gold and could now issue bank notes backed by an "asset" of their choice, which today is governmental debt. Title I and Title IV of the Emergency Act took the Federal Reserve off the gold standard. In 1931, Britain was the first country to drop off the gold standard, and FDR noticed their move to recover. On April 5, 1933, FDR ordered all gold and certificates to be returned to the Federal Reserve. At this time, gold was priced at $20.67 per ounce and by May 10th, they had collected a total of $770 million in gold and certificates. After all the gold was collected, Congress eliminated all gold clauses that required debtors to repay creditors in gold. A year later, the government increased the gold price from $20.67 an ounce to $35 an ounce, which raised their gold reserve value from $770 million to $1.3 billion, giving them more power to inflate the money supply. This was the beginning of the fall of the dollar's buying power, as banks now had the authority to print as much money as they wanted or needed. From 1933 to today, the dollar has depreciated over 97 percent, and we are now facing the same crisis we did during the early 1900s depression. Gold was held at $35 an ounce until August 15th, 1971, when President Nixon announced that the US would no longer convert dollars to gold, which completely removed the United States from the Gold standard globally. In 1974, President Ford signed legislation allowing Americans to own gold again. At the time of this legislation, gold had risen from $35 an ounce to $183.77 an ounce, which would have taken their confiscated gold from a value of $1.3 billion to now $6.8 billion.

Today, the United States' national debt is almost $32 trillion, the total debt is $94 trillion, and the median home price is $448,666, a $200,000 increase from two years ago. If dollars were still attached to gold, gold would be $20,313 an ounce. This should show you how out of control the printing of "fiat money" and government spending has gotten. This is what hidden taxes in the form of inflation looks like. So, how do you survive in a system that confiscates your buying power by the minute? Let's talk about "sound money," ultimately leading you to sound investments.

"History repeats itself, but in such a cunning disguise that we never detect the resemblance until the damage is done." – Sydney Harris.

It is no longer a secret that the history of the early 1900s is now repeating itself in the early 2100s.

Sound Money

The depreciation of our dollars is because it is no longer sound money. Sound money is not liable to sudden appreciation or depreciation and is considered stable. The Federal Reserve tries to create the characteristics of sound money with monetary policy, but it has proven to be impossible with man-made mechanisms of manipulation. For money to be considered sound, it must meet six characteristics shared by the Federal Reserve Bank of St. Louis. The irony is that the institution that is a part of the system educates people on how to differentiate sound money from our "fiat" money even though they do not issue sound money.

To be considered sound, money must have **durability, portability, divisibility, uniformity, limited supply (scarcity), and acceptability**. Let's look at the definition of each of these characteristics and run a checklist on what we think is sound money:

- **Durability** is the ability to withstand wear, pressure, or damage.
- **Portability** is the ability to be easily carried or moved.
- **Divisibility** is the ability to be divided without a remainder.
- **Uniformity** is something of similar form or character to another, fungible.
- **Limited Supply (Scarcity)** is the ability to be restricted in size or amount.
- **Acceptability** is the quality of being tolerated or allowed. The people or users of the currency determine this.

Throughout history, many things have been used as a medium of exchange and as money, but whether it was sound depends on the characteristics we named above. During the bartering age, most monies would be considered commodity money because most of their value was intrinsic. Monies from history include gold, silver, copper, salt, peppercorn, tea, decorated belts, shells, alcohol, cigarettes, silk, candy, nails, cocoa beans, cowries, barley, cattle, and tulips.

If we look at the first characteristic of sound money, we can knock off most of this list. Durability requires that these commodities withstand wear, pressure, or damage, which removes salt, peppercorn, tea, candy, barley, cattle, and tulips from the list. All these commodities have a specific shelf life and will wear down or can be damaged over time. Cattle would have issues with several characteristics like durability, portability, and divisibility. For example, suppose you were bartering and were taking your cattle to be exchanged. In that case, it's possible that your cattle could get sick or tired by the time you make it to your destination for exchange, impacting its durability and portability. Are metals considered sound money? Gold, silver, and copper have the durability to withstand the elements and can be easily carried. However, when it comes to divisibility, they can only be divided to a certain extent. Despite this, metals meet almost all the requirements of sound money and can therefore be considered as such.

The US dollar was considered sound money when it was backed by gold when the United States was on the gold standard. Unfortunately, after President Nixon's administration in 1971, the United States abandoned the gold standard, making the US dollar a fiat currency. The dollar is no longer considered sound money because the government prints notes by the trillions, which means it doesn't have a limited supply. Additionally, the acceptability of the US dollar is questionable, as many are not willing to use it after learning about its value. However, the government still enforces its use as legal tender. So, if the dollar is not sound money, what is it? Fiat currency is a government-issued currency not backed by anything and gives central banks more significant control over the economy. Fiat currency is only acceptable because the government says it is legal tender.

Fiat currency was first introduced in the United States in 1862 when President Abraham Lincoln signed the Legal Tender Act into law. The act allowed the government to print $150 million of unbacked paper notes to fund the Civil War. These notes had to be legitimized by the government because they knew that most people would reject them. The founding fathers of America had this to say about paper money:

"Paper money has had the effect in your state that it will ever have, to ruin commerce, oppress the honest, and open the door to every species of fraud and injustice" – George Washington

"Paper money is liable to abused, has been, is, and forever will be abused, in every country in which it is permitted" – Thomas Jefferson

"The day will come when our Republic will be an impossibility because wealth will be concentrated in the hands of a few. When that day comes, we must rely upon the wisdom of the best elements in the country to readjust the laws of the nation." – James Madison

It is essential to understand the history and characteristics of sound money to navigate the current financial system. Once backed by gold and considered sound money, the US dollar has become a fiat currency subject to inflation and loss of value. The use of paper money as legal tender has a long history of controversy and distrust, yet it remains the primary form of currency used today. Understanding the drawbacks of fiat currency and the characteristics of sound money can empower individuals to make informed decisions about their investments and financial future.

Chapter Three: In Debt, We Trust

"I, however, place economy among the first and most important of virtues, and public debt as the greatest dangers to be feared."

– Thomas Jefferson

In debt, we trust! Debt has become normalized in our society and ingrained in our DNA. Over 120 million American households are in some form of debt, contributing to a total personal household debt of approximately $17 trillion. Studies show that 70% of adults in America have less than $1,000 in their savings accounts, and 40% don't have $400 in their accounts for emergencies. Is this by design? The United States economy has relied on debt since its inception, and the population must remain indebted to keep the system flowing. The Central banks monetized the Federal Reserve Bank Notes, also known as the dollar, with governmental debt through US Treasury bonds. Debt has plagued the United States throughout its history and has become increasingly difficult to control the government.

The United States national debt is currently at $32 trillion, and the government is on the brink of default. If the debt ceiling is not raised for more spending, the government will shut down, and several adverse outcomes will occur. Firstly, interest rates will increase, causing less borrowing and less demand, increasing costs for corporations, government, mortgages, and consumer loans. Secondly, the dollar will drop significantly as foreign investors will no longer see the dollar as a haven. Lastly, the government could not pay salaries or benefits to governmental workers, social security, Medicare, tax refunds, and student loan payments. The banking system would be on the verge of collapse. Banks may resort to a "Bail-In" policy, where they convert deposits into equity, potentially causing the loss of funds for depositors. The United States' debt dates back to 1790, reaching $75 million after the Revolutionary War and growing to $120 million. There has been only one time in American history when the U.S. had no debt, and that was during the Presidency of Andrew Jackson. He was able to bring the debt to zero in 1835. Since then, the debt has risen significantly due to funding seven wars, with the most recent War on Terror costing America $5.9 trillion. In addition, there have been several bank bailouts and trillion-dollar stimulus packages, and we are still adding to the debt.

What does this mean for you? The Central Bank's constant printing of money to pay its bills causes inflation and sometimes hyperinflation, which makes everything around you more expensive even if you haven't received a pay increase at work. The compounding debt in our monetary system is secretly robbing citizens of their wealth. You might be curious about how the government is robbing you of wealth without directly taking from you in plain sight. In James Rickards' book, "The Road to Ruins," he explains the Keynesian Theory perfectly. Economist James Rickards stated that,

"Keynesians embraced the new system because inflation caused by devaluation lowered unit labor costs in real terms. Workers would no longer have to suffer pay cuts. Instead, their wages were stolen through inflation in the expectation that they wouldn't notice until it was too late. Monetarists and Keynesians were now united under the banner of money illusion."

"United under the banner of money illusion" means you are being deceived about what is happening right before you. I wrote this book to decode this money illusion and clearly explain what is happening to you within this system. Once you are informed, you can never be deceived again. The United States dollar has been devaluated since its creation as a note in 1913 when banks were given the authority to back their Federal Reserve Notes with anything in the bank. They chose to back it with governmental debt that gives no reward to the citizen, except devaluation and decreased buying power the longer you keep it in dollar form.

"There are two ways to enslave a nation. One is by the sword, the other by debt."

– John Adams

Today, over 80 percent of Americans are enslaved to a system they have limited understanding of and don't know how to escape. Chapter 4 will delve into how this "SYSTEM" operates. But first, let me ask you a question posed in a famous spoken word called "The Strangest Secret" by Earl Nightingale. Why do you go to work? If your answer is "to pay the bills," congratulations, you are in the system. There's nothing wrong with going to work, but it's essential to understand why you're doing it. Today, people go to work to pay for their basic living needs, pay off debt, and buy things they want. If 80 percent of the population is in debt, then 80 percent must figure out how to make money. If you were in the same school system as I was, you were groomed to work for money rather than getting money to work for you. To be free from this system of debt, you must free yourself from debt to the system. Even in ancient times, such as when Jesus Christ walked the earth, it was understood that whomever you owed a debt to, you were enslaved to them. An old proverb says, "It's better to be the lender and not the borrower" because the borrower becomes a servant to the lender. Whether you believe in God or not, one thing is sure: we were not created to have someone else have dominion over our lives except God.

Total Debt Balance

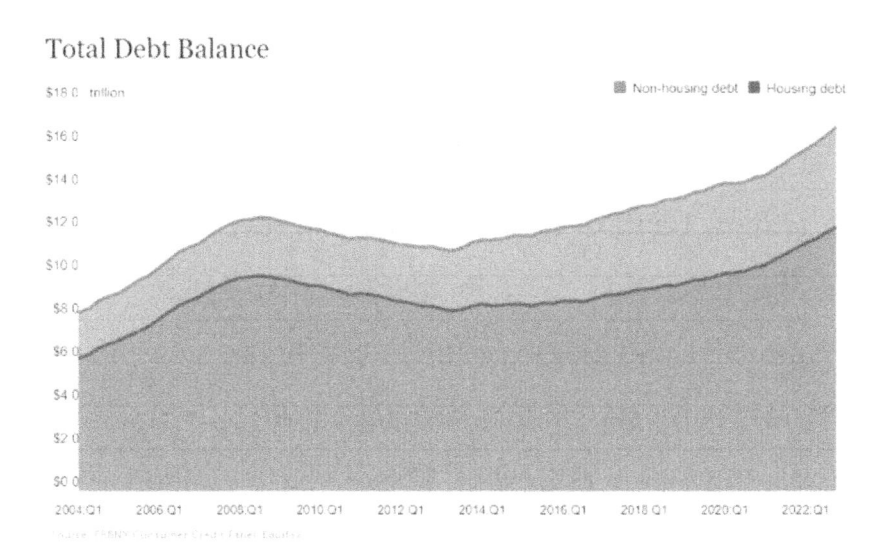

Consumer debt has reached an all-time high of $17 trillion, with student loans leading the way. There can be no debt without credit being extended, and the unfortunate part is that credit is extended to you as soon as you are considered a young adult at 18 years old. One of the most exciting moments of my life was getting my college acceptance letter from Cal State Long Beach, along with how my education would be funded. Like many others, I received a couple of grants, but for the most part, I was stuck with student loans that would be deferred for some years before I could pay them off. Only 1 out of 4 college students will graduate after four years. Most will either take much longer or will not graduate, bringing me to my next point. According to educationdata.org, the average student loan debt is $36,510, and this data considers those who do not graduate as well but still owe the debt to the government. There is a total of 45.3 million people who have accumulated student loan debt, and over half of the borrowers still owe over $20,000 in outstanding debt. Did you know that less than 1 percent of students nationally will receive a full-ride scholarship to college? However, every student coming out of high school looks to get a full-ride scholarship. This is like a casino allowing a couple of people to win to draw in more players, but overall, the casino wins. Colleges are the first place credit is extended to us as young adults, leaving most Americans in debt. Student loans are currently at an all-time high of $1.59 trillion and are the only debt that can't be forgiven. This is our first form of debt provided to us even though we could not intellectually understand the debt and credit system. Why do you think this is? By them indebting you early, it increases the likelihood of enslaving you to my work system. Once you are enslaved, you must work to pay off your debt, which means you must pay taxes since you're working. That's why the Federal Reserve's top priority is to maximize employment. Why do they need to maximize employment? Because when people are employed, they pay TAXES. How does the government make money?! YES, through TAXES. This system is built around you paying taxes to create revenue for the government, and you are targeted before you even know better.

Mortgage debt is the most significant debt held by Americans, with the total debt in the 2nd quarter reaching $10.4 trillion nationwide. According to usdebtclock.org, the median home price has risen from $255,000 to $448,666. The Federal Reserve, as of 2021, dropped interest rates to their lowest point possible to get more Americans to borrow more money. However, despite low loan rates, most Americans, who represented the median income, still couldn't afford to buy a home at its median cost. The median income nationwide, as represented on usdebtclock.org, is $35,782, which, when broken down, is $2,971 monthly. A home at $448,666 with taxes and insurance will be approximately $4,000 monthly, making this unattainable for the average person in America. The average American will pay over $280,000 in interest, with a majority contributing to home ownership. Nerd Wallet reported that Americans' average monthly car payment in 2021 was $575, with an average borrowed amount of $35,163.

However, in the past year, car payments have risen, and the average now stands at $716, with the average car purchase costing around $50,000.

The last item on our list is consumer credit card debt, which is at an all-time high of $998.4 billion in total debt. The average American has at least four credit cards; according to creditcards.com, the average balance is $5,525. Almost 70 percent of Americans with credit card balances keep a revolving credit, meaning they keep a balance on their card that accumulates interest charges. Of that 70 percent, about 25 percent went dormant, meaning they could not pay or were in a delinquent status, which, according to creditcards.com, rose from 10 percent primarily due to the pandemic in 2020. The average credit interest percentage ranges between 16.20 to 24 percent, meaning that for every dollar that carries over to the next month, you'll pay 16 to 24 cents per dollar. So, if you have $1,000 as a revolving balance, each day, you will have interest charges added to your balance based on the daily rate, which is found by dividing your average per year (APY) percentage by 365 days. For example, if you had a 24.6 percent APY, you would divide that by 365 days, which would equal .06 percent daily, so on a balance of $1,000, you would pay 0.67 cents daily starting, but over time that percentage rate compounds, which charges you more than the percentage you are presented. Simple math would make you think that if you kept a $1,000 balance at 24.6 percent, you would only pay $246 in total interest by the end of the year. However, with it compounding daily, your total interest at the end of the year would be $364. You are paying 36 percent of what you borrowed, and this doesn't include late fees.

The world has come a long way in extending credit and debt to the public. Extending public credit wasn't normal in America, and issuing credit was considered very risky. From 1800 to 1900, if credit was extended to citizens, it was usually only extended for home purchases and no more than 3-6 years max with variable interest rates, with the average monthly payment being $7-11.00. We've come a long way from paying $7 monthly for a mortgage to several thousand. Our current credit system is less than a century old, and some systems that were created are less than 50 years old, meaning we are still learning the impact. Between 1900 and 1960, several things were introduced to the nation, including the first credit bureau birthed out of Atlanta. Henry Ford invented one of the first automobiles in America, and initially, he didn't extend credit but allowed Americans to place their car on layaway. However, this posed a problem, as people made monthly payments for a car they didn't yet have. Later, Mr. Ford started extending internal credit for customers to buy his cars without paying in full. In 1938, Fannie Mae was created to connect borrowers to lenders, allowing for more homeownership. The first credit card, the "Diner Club" card, was created in 1950, and it was similar to an American Express card today as the balance had to be paid off every month. In 1951, the first bank credit card was introduced, and by 1953, over 60 credit card plans were available to citizens. Banks saw the profitability in extending credit and started allowing consumers to keep a revolving balance on their cards, thereby earning interest paid monthly. As we evolved into a country that would extend credit to its citizens, we had to build an infrastructure around this lucrative business model. In 1968, TRW Information Systems, now known as Transunion and Experian, was created to collect data from consumers using credit. In 1970, legislation was passed to regulate the industry.

Looking at all forms of debt that most of the nation has been conditioned to hold, gaining financial freedom can seem impossible. The constant calls from collection agencies can be overwhelming, and citizens cannot pay off their debt due to job losses and other issues. Most people don't realize that the longer they are exposed to this credit-debt-driven system, the more money they will likely tie up in long-term interest costs. This book contains strategies to help you pay off your debt, recover the interest you've been paying creditors, and build wealth.

Imagine being debt-free today and owing no one. How would that feel? You would likely feel a significant weight lifted off your shoulders and experience freedom from the stress of creditors constantly calling. Financial problems are typically at the center of most marriages, and while they may not be the primary contributor to divorce, they certainly contribute. Currently, in America, 50 percent of marriages end in divorce. The combined median household income is approximately $57,000 yearly, with two working adults. Still, most Americans make less than $30,000 a year and cannot sustain their basic needs. The worst part is that the government cannot pay its bills, causing them to look for more ways to tax citizens without their knowledge. The show has almost stopped, as there is no more money to squeeze out of hard-working citizens.

We have seen how the American credit system has evolved, from the days of layaway plans to the creation of credit cards and the birth of credit bureaus. However, this system has also led to a culture of debt and constant financial struggles for many Americans. We have also explored the different forms of debt most citizens hold and their long-term impact on their financial well-being. But there is hope. In the following chapters, we will delve deeper into the "SYSTEM" and uncover ways to break free from the bondage of debt and accumulate wealth. It is time to take control of your finances and secure a brighter future for you and your family.

Chapter Four: The System

"You have to understand most of these people are not ready to be unplugged. And many of them are so inured, so hopelessly dependent on the system that they will fight to protect it."
– *Morpheus (The Matrix)*

The 1999 movie series "The Matrix" featured a famous question posed by the character Morpheus, played by Lawrence Fishburne. He asked whether one would prefer the "Red pill" or the "Blue pill." This question has since become a viral sensation, often accompanied by a meme of Morpheus with this saying attached. However, the question holds a deeper meaning. In the movie, Morpheus presented the protagonist Neo, played by Keanu Reeves, with two options - to take the "Red pill" and learn the truth about the Matrix, or to take the "Blue pill" and return to his former life, knowing nothing.

Concerning financial independence, one must also ask oneself where one stands. To attain this goal, it is essential to challenge what has been taught about the money and banking system. Similar to "The Matrix", everyday life often involves doing things without fully understanding the reasons behind them.

For example, it is a common belief that obtaining more education leads to increased earnings. However, this often leads to more debt, and if the career being pursued does not pay significantly more than the previous job, it may not be a good return on investment. According to the Washington Post, only 27% of college graduates have a job related to their major. Furthermore, 39% of those with 2-4-year degrees do not believe attending college was worthwhile, according to a survey conducted by the same source. Another study by finder.com found that 43.7% of graduates between 22-27 years old are underemployed and not working in their field of study, while 34.4% of all graduates between the ages of 22-65 years old are underemployed. Why do graduates struggle to find acceptable employment? An article broke down seven reasons: (1) high competition, (2) lack of work experience, (3) few or no skills, (4) little networking, (5) lack of follow-up, (6) lack of communication skills, and (7) uncertainty with major. Let's focus on the first two: high competition, which translates into too many people and too few jobs available in that field, placing the power in the employer's hands to set labor costs. This is simple supply and demand, which means if there is high demand for employment in your field, you'll likely accept a lower wage, enter another field of employment, or remain unemployed.

Only 20.3 percent of all college students graduate annually. However, the system of obtaining a college education is still being pushed regardless of the findings or consequences. Why? Because it generates revenue for the system. Currently, colleges nationwide employ about 3.6 million people, and approximately 20 million students are enrolled in college across the country. If there were no colleges, there would be 3.6 million unemployed people and 20 million people looking for some form of employment instead of attending college. While we need college for advanced careers like being a doctor, lawyer, or engineer, it shouldn't be a degree if it doesn't pertain to a specific field.

    This pill is hard to swallow for most because attending college has been ingrained in us since the beginning of our school journey. We romanticize the college experience and culture without ever considering if we need college. As a result, most Americans enter college uncertain about what they want to do and leave with college loan debt that they cannot repay. However, as we mentioned in earlier chapters, once a citizen is in debt, they must work to pay off their debt, and if they must work, they must pay taxes. Taxes are how the government generates revenue. The more taxpayers, the more revenue the government generates.

There is a saying that I believe is an excellent motto for our monetary system: "If it doesn't make dollars, then it doesn't make sense." Everything the government puts in place is to create more revenue for the government, not the people. To fully understand the system, there are three mandates that the US Congress placed on the Federal Reserve to promote: (1) maximum employment, (2) stable prices, and (3) moderate long-term interest. So, how does the Federal Reserve accomplish these mandates, and how does it impact you?

Promote Maximum Employment

The Federal Reserve is tasked with the dual mandate of promoting a strong US economy, which requires using a monetary policy tool called Quantitative easing. The Feds use this tool to purchase long-term securities, typically treasury bonds, with newly printed bank reserves to increase the money supply and promote lending. Purchasing these securities adds money to the economy, lowering interest rates due to the bid-up of fixed securities. The central bank places these treasury bonds on its balance sheet before lending them to the public. At this point, a US dollar is not considered money until borrowed from the bank. Therefore, the central banking system is essentially buying labor, as individuals must borrow money and work to pay for it, thus creating more money and paying taxes to the government.

      To achieve maximum employment, the Federal Reserve lowers interest rates, making it cheaper for businesses to borrow money. The belief is that when money is cheaper to borrow, businesses will use it to expand their operations and hire more employees. According to the Federal Reserve, maximum employment is the highest or lowest level of unemployment that can be achieved and sustained in an economy while maintaining stable inflation rates. However, the dual mandate gets tricky as it is counterintuitive to maintaining stable prices. Lowering interest rates and printing trillions of dollars causes inflation, driving up prices. The Federal Reserve must balance promoting maximum employment and stable prices, which is difficult, particularly during a depression. Promoting maximum employment and stable prices are the most critical mandates that the Federal Reserve has. The more citizens in the workforce, the more taxpayers there are to create revenue for the government.

Promote Stable Prices

The Federal Reserve utilizes open market operations to promote stable prices by adjusting the supply of reserves. This involves printing money and purchasing treasury bonds, which are then added to the balance sheet and injected into the economy. Before March 2020, the Federal Reserve controlled stable prices by tightening or loosening reserves for banks. When reserves were scarce, this created a stable level of demand that increased the federal funds rate. Conversely, abundant reserves allowed banks to loan more and lower interest rates to attract borrowers. However, in March 2020, reserve requirements were eliminated for all depository institutions, allowing them to loan out every cent held in the bank. As a result, digital money creation is infinite until the Federal Reserve reintroduces reserves and increases interest rates to slow down inflation. Tightening the money supply during the current depression would be detrimental to the American economy, as money needs to circulate continuously through the economy to stimulate growth. Therefore, the Federal Reserve must keep money accessible to support economic recovery.

Product	Price 2020	Price 2021	Price % Increase
Gas (Dallas, TX)	$2.32	$3.69	59%
Gas (Los Angeles)	$3.42	$4.37	27%
Gas (New York)	$2.17	$3.21	48%

Figure 4 True inflation measure by gas prices from 2020 – 2021

Currently, stable prices are spiraling out of control due to ineffective quantitative easing measures applied by the Federal Reserve. Inflation is commonly determined through the Consumer Price Index (CPI), which is reported by the Bureau of Labor Statistics. However, there is much controversy surrounding how it is being reported. Some believe that the CPI is being underestimated regarding inflation, as the basket of consumer goods used to measure inflation can be subjective. In Figure 4, we present the actual numbers of inflation measured on a daily use resource, gasoline, in three major cities. These numbers show that we have a higher inflation rate than we think. If government agencies are willing to manipulate a number about inflation, it raises the question of what else can be manipulated.

Gasoline prices in major cities like Dallas, Los Angeles, and New York from 2020 to 2021 indicate an average inflation rate of 44 percent, which could be closer to 50 percent. This brings up an important question - are we experiencing hyperinflation? Hyperinflation is characterized by rapid, excessive, and out-of-control price increases in the economy. It is typically measured when inflation is more than 50 percent per month. Due to low-interest rates and the constant printing of Federal Reserve Notes, we are on our way to a hyperinflation scenario as the economy is not responding to the typical tools used to stimulate it.

To succeed in an inflationary environment, you must own goods, services, or assets that increase with inflation. Your buying power will decrease daily if you lack an asset that counters inflation.

Promote Long-Term Interest Rates

When the Federal Reserve reaches a point where inflation is manageable, it can focus on its final mandate of setting long-term interest rates. However, as explained in previous paragraphs, the economy is currently far from being able to run on autopilot. Figure 4 breaks down how to accurately measure inflation concerning household goods and services. For instance, if a household rents and operates two cars, they will feel the impact of inflation more than a household that owns their home and only has one car. The cost of gas and real estate, both subject to inflation, will consume a more significant percentage of their monthly rent. Conversely, a household with assets like cryptocurrency, real estate, and/or businesses selling goods/services that rise with inflation will benefit from increased wealth.

It is, therefore, crucial to understand the true nature of inflation and how it affects individuals. According to an article in Forbes magazine by Chase Peterson-Withorn, during the Covid-19 pandemic, 650 billionaires increased their wealth by 35 percent, generating a record $1.2 trillion, while simultaneously, 20 million Americans lost their jobs. This raises the question of how this wealth gap can exist during a crisis that affects the entire population.

The Federal Reserve's mandates to promote maximum employment, stable prices, and long-term interest rates are crucial to maintaining a strong US economy. While the current situation is challenging, understanding the impact of inflation and how it affects individuals can help people make informed decisions to protect their finances and assets. The wealth gap highlighted during the Covid-19 pandemic underscores the importance of analyzing the underlying mechanisms of the economy and striving for a more equitable distribution of wealth.

Inflation Discriminates

Inflation is a phenomenon that has a discriminatory effect on the poor and benefits the rich. However, before you start blaming the system for your lack of wealth, it is essential to understand why inflation disproportionately affects the poor. While inflation picks winners and losers in the economy, the good news is that you can choose which side you rest on. Inflation occurs when prices increase and the purchasing power of money decreases. If you don't own any assets, you must pay more for the things you use. For example, when gas prices increased by 44-60 percent, it enormously impacted families who commuted to work and did not receive a pay raise. If you used to pay $50 weekly for gas, you are likely paying double the cost, around $100-110 weekly. This sudden expense increase is significant and can lead to financial hardships for many families. Unfortunately, during inflation, the only thing that typically doesn't go up is labor cost, so most people feel the impact of inflation.

However, if you owned a gas station or were in the oil industry, then you benefited from the increase in fuel prices. During times of inflation, spenders are losers, and investors are winners. Inflation devours wealth in families before they even see it coming. This phenomenon can be compared to the old fable of the boiling frog, where a frog can be boiled alive in a pot that they didn't realize was being heated until it was too late. Inflation does the same to average working families who don't understand the monetary system. The frog metaphor represents how inflation can entirely eat up a family's paycheck and wealth-building potential over time if they don't own anything that moves up with inflation. The slow boil represents every year that the goods and services your family utilizes go up in cost while your hourly wage stays the same. You are the frog in the pot, the pot represents the economy, and the water represents the system. Many people are starting to realize that the money they've saved for years in their retirement is not enough to retire in this new economy. They've boiled slowly, and now it's too late.

Inflation is a hidden taxation on people, and it has been weaponized over the past 100 years by our central banking system. It is an attack on your family's wealth; the only way to beat it is to understand how it's created. The first step in combating inflation is to turn your money into sound money. We can teach you how to do this by showing you how to back it with an asset that will move up with inflation, such as cryptocurrency, real estate, or a business that sells goods/services that increase with inflation.

It is crucial to understand what inflation truly is and how it impacts your financial well-being. According to an article written in Forbes magazine by Chase Peterson-Withorn, during the Covid-19 pandemic, 650 billionaires increased their wealth by 35 percent, bringing in a record of $1.2 trillion, while at the same time, 20 million Americans were losing their jobs. This inequality results from rigging the system favoring those who understand how to leverage assets to combat inflation.

In summary, inflation discriminates against the poor and favors the rich. But, with the proper knowledge and tools, you can protect yourself and your family from its harmful effects. Understanding the monetary system, how inflation works, and owning assets that move up with inflation is vital to building wealth and financial stability. Don't be the frog in the boiling pot; take action now to secure your financial future.

Inflation is Manufactured

In the current monetary system, certain groups have organized themselves into what can be referred to as cartels to control supply, demand, and pricing. These groups have gained the ability to control the choke points of supply and, by doing so, have the power to manufacture demand and ultimately control prices. Cartels, as defined, are organizations of suppliers to maintain high prices and stifle competition. These are the same associations formed over the years in our monetary system, from banking to infrastructure to oil. The world has been deceived into believing that it's in their best interest that their money affairs are managed by a central authority. These groups have taken advantage of their control over supply to benefit themselves.

Understanding supply and demand is essential to understanding how it affects us today. When there is a limited supply of something and a higher demand for it, prices will likely increase due to the demand and limited amount. Manipulating the market by limiting supply is an age-old practice still used today by some businesses dealing with rare art, designer clothing, shoes, or rare collectible cars. If you were the only producer of a high-demand product, you would be considered a monopoly because of your dominant position in that industry, allowing you to control pricing and competition. The United States has Antitrust laws enacted to regulate the practices of businesses to promote competition and prevent monopoly, but these laws do not apply to government-backed institutions.

It is evident that in our current monetary system, organized groups have taken control and have used their position to benefit themselves. As individuals, we must understand the workings of supply and demand to make informed decisions about our finances. Being aware of the manipulation that can occur in the market is crucial to making sound financial decisions.

Business practices where organizations band together to coordinate pricing and supply raise many flags. The Organization of Petroleum Exporting Countries (OPEC) was formed in the 1960s to control the supply and pricing of oil. According to their mission statement on their site, "the mission of the Organization of the Petroleum Exporting Countries (OPEC) is to coordinate and unify the petroleum policies of its member countries and ensure the stabilization of oil markets to secure an efficient, economical, and regular supply of petroleum to consumers, a steady income to producers, and a fair return on capital for those investing in the petroleum industry."

While each country must handle its affairs and economy, businesses are in business to make profits. According to OPEC's mission statement, its mission is to ensure adequate profits for all participating members. Just last year, at the beginning of 2020, Russia did not want to cut its oil supply as OPEC suggested. At that time, there was an ample supply of oil, which allowed prices to decrease at a respectable rate. However, after some pressure from all the OPEC member countries, Russia eventually agreed to cut the oil production supply in half. This single manipulation of oil production increased the price of fuel globally. Unfortunately, this is not a free market operation but central control and legalized supply manipulation.

This example of how price is manipulated based on supply is similar to what happens with our money source provided by the Federal Reserve. Inflation is manufactured when the Federal Reserve applies quantitative easing by lowering interest rates and injecting more Federal Reserve Notes into the economy. If this monetary policy of QE is applied over a long period, we will eventually go into hyperinflation, causing prices to increase over 50 percent in one month or buying power to decrease by 50 percent. Quantitative easing (QE) occurs when the Federal Reserve purchases US Treasury bonds or governmental debt on the open market to inject new money into the economy. In short, QE means that the Federal Reserve prints money and then buys Treasury bonds to place on their balance sheet as an asset to issue loans to their member banks to loan out to the public. Our money is backed by governmental debt bought by the Federal Reserve and placed on their balance sheet as an asset. It is considered an asset because they receive interest upon maturity of the debt it bought from the government. The Federal Reserve controls the expansion and contraction of the economy by increasing or decreasing assets and liabilities on its balance sheet.

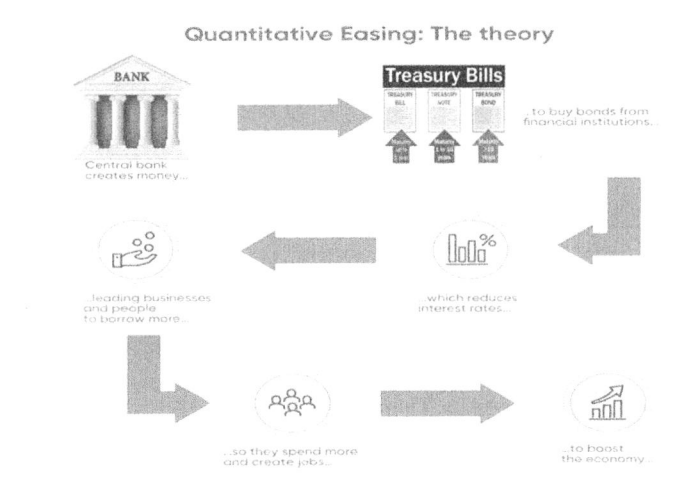

Quantitative Easing: The theory

As of the writing of this book, the government currently owes the Federal Reserve $3.4 trillion in interest per year, and the only way for the government to continue to pay this is to create revenue. The government only makes revenue from one stream: taxes. This brings us back to the importance of the first mandate. The Federal Reserve must promote maximum employment so that more people are in the workforce and are paying taxes. To create maximum employment, the Federal Reserve must expand the economy by injecting more money back into the economy by buying Treasury notes/bonds, which will lower interest rates to make money cheaper for businesses to borrow and expand their operations. At the same time, this causes inflation of goods and services and creates more interest for the Federal Reserve. Expanding the economy and buying more assets places them in the position to receive more interest.

However, this is one of the issues that the monetary system is dealing with today as the usual monetary policy of QE is not expanding the workforce, which in turn is not increasing government revenue. When the government cannot increase its revenue through maximizing employment, the next option is increasing taxes on those who can pay. The government keeps a real-time account of the debt and taxes owed by each citizen. According to www.debtclock.org, based on our current national debt, each taxpayer would be responsible for $228,999 as of October

2021, expected to increase to $358,396 by 2025. This is clearly unattainable for most people, especially considering the median income is only $35,678. This leads to the question of who will ultimately bear the burden of this debt. It's a never-ending cycle that continually depletes the people's wealth through hidden taxation called inflation.

So, how can you combat inflation and protect your family's buying power? To thrive in this monetary system based on debt and spending, you must place yourself in a position that benefits from inflation. You must become the lender over the borrower and the investor over the spender. In a long-term inflationary environment, wealth requires investing in assets that increase in value over time, such as real estate, stocks, or owning a business with services that increase in price over time.

Fortunately, a new financial class is proving to be an excellent solution for families willing to learn about it. Later chapters will show you how to leverage the current financial system and the digital asset market to back your money and create your banking system.

Chapter Five: The 401k Fugazi

"In the long run, the most unpleasant truth is a safer companion than a pleasant falsehood."
– Theodore Roosevelt

Retirement planning is a common concern for individuals who hope to leave the workforce and live comfortably with financial stability. Unfortunately, recent data from the Bureau of Labor Statistics indicates that only 50% of Americans have access to a retirement or pension plan offered by their employers. Even among those participating in such plans, over half have not accumulated enough savings to retire comfortably. In today's world, many individuals find retirement a distant and unattainable dream. Value Penguin's research suggests that six out of ten Americans aged 60-67 do not have sufficient retirement savings, leaving many seniors dependent on government assistance to make ends meet. It raises the question: were Americans sold an inflated dream that they could work for 30-40 years, retire, and still have enough money to live comfortably? Recent studies suggest that retirement plans such as the 401K, first introduced in the United States in

1979, were oversold to the public. The truth may have been stretched to convince clients they could accumulate enough money to retire after 40 years of work.

A simple online search on retirement savings advice reveals a wealth of information, much of which provides similar guidance. For instance, Teachers Insurance and Annuity of America (TIAA) advises individuals to consider saving 10-15% of their income and suggests that using a 401K plan with an employer match could reduce this to 5%. Many employees accept this advice without realizing that it may not be sufficient. It's essential to take a closer look at the numbers. SmartMoney.com says the average annual return for a 401K portfolio is 5-8%. Similarly, Fidelity recommends that individuals save at least 15% of their income, including the employer match. However, the fees associated with these retirement plans are not often discussed in these conversations. In a later section, we will address these hidden fees. But for now, consider an example: a person earning $63,000 annually who contributes 15% of their income to a retirement plan yielding 8% annually.

Years	401K contribution	Interest growth	Total Balance	Annual contributions
1	$ 9,500.00	$ 760.00	$ 10,260.00	
2	$ 19,760.00	$ 1,580.80	$ 21,340.80	$ 9,500.00
3	$ 30,840.80	$ 2,467.26	$ 33,308.06	$ 9,500.00
4	$ 42,808.06	$ 3,424.65	$ 46,232.71	$ 9,500.00
5	$ 55,732.71	$ 4,458.62	$ 60,191.33	$ 9,500.00
6	$ 69,691.33	$ 5,575.31	$ 75,266.63	$ 9,500.00
7	$ 84,766.63	$ 6,781.33	$ 91,547.96	$ 9,500.00
8	$ 101,047.96	$ 8,083.84	$ 109,131.80	$ 9,500.00
9	$ 118,631.80	$ 9,490.54	$ 128,122.34	$ 9,500.00
10	$ 137,622.34	$ 11,009.79	$ 148,632.13	$ 9,500.00
11	$ 158,132.13	$ 12,650.57	$ 170,782.70	$ 9,500.00
12	$ 180,282.70	$ 14,422.62	$ 194,705.32	$ 9,500.00
13	$ 204,205.32	$ 16,336.43	$ 220,541.74	$ 9,500.00
14	$ 230,041.74	$ 18,403.34	$ 248,445.08	$ 9,500.00
15	$ 257,945.08	$ 20,635.61	$ 278,580.69	$ 9,500.00
16	$ 288,080.69	$ 23,046.46	$ 311,127.14	$ 9,500.00
17	$ 320,627.14	$ 25,650.17	$ 346,277.32	$ 9,500.00
18	$ 355,777.32	$ 28,462.19	$ 384,239.50	$ 9,500.00
19	$ 393,739.50	$ 31,499.16	$ 425,238.66	$ 9,500.00
20	$ 434,738.66	$ 34,779.09	$ 469,517.75	$ 9,500.00
21	$ 479,017.75	$ 38,321.42	$ 517,339.17	$ 9,500.00
22	$ 526,839.17	$ 42,147.13	$ 568,986.31	$ 9,500.00
23	$ 578,486.31	$ 46,278.90	$ 624,765.21	$ 9,500.00
24	$ 634,265.21	$ 50,741.22	$ 685,006.43	$ 9,500.00
25	$ 694,506.43	$ 55,560.51	$ 750,066.94	$ 9,500.00
26	$ 759,566.94	$ 60,765.36	$ 820,332.30	$ 9,500.00
27	$ 829,832.30	$ 66,386.58	$ 896,218.88	$ 9,500.00
28	$ 905,718.88	$ 72,457.51	$ 978,176.39	$ 9,500.00
29	$ 987,676.39	$ 79,014.11	$ 1,066,690.51	$ 9,500.00
30	$ 1,076,190.51	$ 86,095.24	$ 1,162,285.75	$ 9,500.00
TOTAL		$ 877,285.75		$ 275,500.00

The preceding chart illustrates the potential outcome of investing $9,500 annually in a 401K, assuming a perfect scenario and ideal conditions. According to Business Insider, the average salary of a public school teacher is $63,645. As such, we have based our example on this statistic and assumed the highest recommended contribution of 15%. In an ideal situation, i.e., no market crashes, optimal portfolio management, and an annual account growth rate of 8% with no losses, your total 401K portfolio would amount to $1,162,285. This sum is derived from a total contribution of $275,500, yielding growth and profit of $877,285.

However, it is essential to consider and factor in all the hidden variables that can impact the bottom line of a 401K retirement plan. These factors include hidden fees, market fluctuations, interest rates, inflation, and the amount of annual investment. In the previous example, we intentionally omitted the hidden fees that 401K plan providers charge monthly to manage your retirement account. In reality, the impact of these fees on your compounded principal balance over 30 years can be significant. To put it into perspective, for every dollar of monthly fees applied, it would cost you approximately $4-5 of your retirement savings.

Hidden Fees

According to CNBC and Investopedia, the average hidden fees for managing 401(K) plans range from 0.5% to 2% per year. The chart below will demonstrate how these fees can affect your retirement savings before taxes. Our previous example showed that contributing 15% of a teacher's annual salary under perfect conditions can yield a retirement balance of just over $1.1 million. However, when the standard 2% yearly fees are applied to the same example retirement plan, the balance drops to $772,880, a decrease of $389,405 from the previous balance without fees. These fees can significantly impact the 401(K) plan, primarily due to missed opportunities to compound the charged money monthly. The total fees charged in this example were $176,839 to manage the 401(K) account. However, since this amount was not part of the compounding equation, it led to missed income opportunities of $212,566. According to a recent Business Insider article, the average 401(K) plan balance is $106,478, and the median 401(K) plan balance is $25,775, according to Vanguard's 2020 analysis.

Years	401K contribution	Interest growth	Total Balance	Annual contributions	fees %	Fee cost	No fees
1	$ 9,500.00	$ 760.00	$ 10,054.80		2%	$ 201.10	$ 10,260.00
2	$ 19,554.80	$ 1,564.38	$ 20,696.80	$ 9,500.00	2%	$ 413.94	$ 21,340.80
3	$ 30,196.80	$ 2,415.74	$ 31,960.29	$ 9,500.00	2%	$ 639.21	$ 33,308.06
4	$ 41,460.29	$ 3,316.82	$ 43,881.57	$ 9,500.00	2%	$ 877.63	$ 46,232.71
5	$ 53,381.57	$ 4,270.53	$ 56,499.06	$ 9,500.00	2%	$ 1,129.98	$ 60,191.33
6	$ 65,999.06	$ 5,279.92	$ 69,853.40	$ 9,500.00	2%	$ 1,397.07	$ 75,266.63
7	$ 79,353.40	$ 6,348.27	$ 83,987.64	$ 9,500.00	2%	$ 1,679.75	$ 91,547.96
8	$ 93,487.64	$ 7,479.01	$ 98,947.32	$ 9,500.00	2%	$ 1,978.95	$ 109,131.80
9	$ 108,447.32	$ 8,675.79	$ 114,780.64	$ 9,500.00	2%	$ 2,295.61	$ 128,122.34
10	$ 124,280.64	$ 9,942.45	$ 131,538.63	$ 9,500.00	2%	$ 2,630.77	$ 148,632.13
11	$ 141,038.63	$ 11,283.09	$ 149,275.29	$ 9,500.00	2%	$ 2,985.51	$ 170,782.70
12	$ 158,775.29	$ 12,702.02	$ 168,047.77	$ 9,500.00	2%	$ 3,360.96	$ 194,705.32
13	$ 177,547.77	$ 14,203.82	$ 187,916.56	$ 9,500.00	2%	$ 3,758.33	$ 220,541.74
14	$ 197,416.56	$ 15,793.32	$ 208,945.68	$ 9,500.00	2%	$ 4,178.91	$ 248,445.08
15	$ 218,445.68	$ 17,475.65	$ 231,202.91	$ 9,500.00	2%	$ 4,624.06	$ 278,580.69
16	$ 240,702.91	$ 19,256.23	$ 254,759.96	$ 9,500.00	2%	$ 5,095.20	$ 311,127.14
17	$ 264,259.96	$ 21,140.80	$ 279,692.74	$ 9,500.00	2%	$ 5,593.85	$ 346,277.32
18	$ 289,192.74	$ 23,135.42	$ 306,081.60	$ 9,500.00	2%	$ 6,121.63	$ 384,239.50
19	$ 315,581.60	$ 25,246.53	$ 334,011.56	$ 9,500.00	2%	$ 6,680.23	$ 425,238.66
20	$ 343,511.56	$ 27,480.93	$ 363,572.64	$ 9,500.00	2%	$ 7,271.45	$ 469,517.75
21	$ 373,072.64	$ 29,845.81	$ 394,860.08	$ 9,500.00	2%	$ 7,897.20	$ 517,339.17
22	$ 404,360.08	$ 32,348.81	$ 427,974.71	$ 9,500.00	2%	$ 8,559.49	$ 568,986.31
23	$ 437,474.71	$ 34,997.98	$ 463,023.23	$ 9,500.00	2%	$ 9,260.46	$ 624,765.21
24	$ 472,523.23	$ 37,801.86	$ 500,118.59	$ 9,500.00	2%	$ 10,002.37	$ 685,006.43
25	$ 509,618.59	$ 40,769.49	$ 539,380.32	$ 9,500.00	2%	$ 10,787.61	$ 750,066.94
26	$ 548,880.32	$ 43,910.43	$ 580,934.93	$ 9,500.00	2%	$ 11,618.70	$ 820,332.30
27	$ 590,434.93	$ 47,234.79	$ 624,916.33	$ 9,500.00	2%	$ 12,498.33	$ 896,218.88
28	$ 634,416.33	$ 50,753.31	$ 671,466.24	$ 9,500.00	2%	$ 13,429.32	$ 978,176.39
29	$ 680,966.24	$ 54,477.30	$ 720,734.67	$ 9,500.00	2%	$ 14,414.69	$ 1,066,690.51
30	$ 730,234.67	$ 58,418.77	$ 772,880.37	$ 9,500.00	2%	$ 15,457.61	$ 1,162,285.75
TOTAL		$ 668,329.28		$ 275,500.00		$ 176,839.93	

It is evident that a significant number of people are not prepared for retirement, even after reaching retirement age. Unfortunately, the current monetary system does not provide much help either, especially if most individuals utilizing the system do not understand it. Over 45 percent of baby boomers at retirement age have no retirement savings. Of the remaining 55 percent with retirement savings, 28 percent have less than $10,000 saved up, according to recent statistics from the US

Census Bureau. Additionally, about 10,000 baby boomers turn 65 every day, and by 2030, all baby boomers will be over 65. As a result, this will significantly impact the economy as more baby boomers enter retirement age with little to no retirement savings, putting more burden on social security benefits, which we will discuss later in this chapter. It is worth noting that the government only has a few options to fix this problem, namely, (1) reducing expenses, (2) increasing taxes, or (3) printing more money to cover the expenses. This leads us to the next major factor that impacts your retirement: inflation and taxes.

The Impact of Inflation on Your Retirement Plan

Inflation is often misunderstood by those who lack an understanding of economics, yet its impact on retirement cannot be overstated. Inflation occurs when the cost of goods and services increases or the currency's buying power decreases. According to policymakers, a healthy inflation rate is 2 percent, which is one of the mandates placed on the Federal Reserve to promote stable prices and long-term interest. Failure to account for inflation when planning for retirement can have severe consequences. Goods and services you currently use and will continue to use after retirement will cost much more after several years of inflation.

As of the time of writing, the United States national debt is at $32 trillion and is estimated to reach $84 trillion within the next eight years, according to the US Debt Clock. This means that a significant amount of money will be printed, or in financial terms, there will be a quantitative easing of the economy. The more money printed or entered into circulation, the more your buying power will decrease, leading to inflation.

To illustrate how inflation can impact retirement, let's consider some expenses that retirees typically face, such as gas, rent/mortgage, utility bills, medical insurance, and possibly a new vehicle. In just the past year, the average price of gasoline across the United States has increased from $2.17 to over $3.38, representing a 56 percent increase. If you previously spent $100 a week on gas, you now need to budget $156 weekly and $624 monthly, which adds $224 per month to your expenses. Similarly, rental and housing markets have seen significant price increases, with home values projected to increase by 25 percent in the next 4 years and 55 percent in 8 years. This is excellent news for those who own their homes but may be a significant challenge for renters who will likely face rent increases of 25-50 percent. The average rent cost in the United States is around $1200, but with a 50 percent increase, renters could look at $1800-2000 a month. For someone retiring in the next ten years who doesn't own a home, this expense can easily change the amount of retirement savings they will require.

Inflation is a silent killer of fiat currency, and it must be an essential element to pay attention to when building wealth. Failure to account for inflation when planning for retirement can have dire consequences. To combat inflation, you must become inflation-proof by owning things that increase in value with inflation, such as real estate, or by leveraging real estate, life insurance contracts, and cryptocurrency to hedge against economic instability.

"By a continuing process of inflation, the government can confiscate, secretly and unobserved, an important part of the wealth of their citizens."

- John Maynard Keynes

The Impact of Taxes on Your Retirement Plan

One of the primary selling points of a 401(K) plan is the ability to invest money before paying taxes and then pay taxes on that money when withdrawing it in retirement. However, the benefit of paying taxes later depends on your current tax bracket and where you expect to end up. Tax situations can vary widely between individuals, especially for those in higher tax brackets. If you expect to earn more in retirement than you currently do, paying taxes later may not be your best option. Assuming that tax rates will remain the same over the next 30 to 40 years is not a safe bet, and taxes will likely increase as the government works to address its debts. Taxes are the primary means by which the government generates revenue, so raising taxes may be necessary for the future. Whether you pay taxes now or later doesn't matter, as it's uncertain whether tax rates will be higher or lower. What's important to understand is that taxes will significantly impact your retirement, depending on how much income you withdraw each year.

In our example of a teacher's 401(K) retirement plan, if they plan to withdraw the same amount of annual income earned before retirement, they could expect to pay at least 12 percent in taxes based on current tax rules. This would decrease their retirement portfolio by another $100,000. When factoring in fees, inflation, and taxes, over half of the retirement portfolio could be lost, even after 30 years of diligent contributions.

According to the American Academy of Actuaries, most tax provisions affecting retirement plans do not typically impact the long-term increase or decrease of tax revenue. The tax difference provided by a 401(K) is not always a benefit if the participant is still subject to the same tax rates when they made their contributions. Therefore, it's crucial to account for fees, inflation, and taxes when planning for retirement and to educate yourself on the nuances of retirement planning rather than accepting advice at face value.

The Impact of Governmental Legislation on f-Retirement plans

Legislation can significantly impact retirement plans, and it is crucial to understand its influence during the wealth creation process. While some legislation may appear beneficial for retirement plans, history has shown that many bills have been used to transfer wealth from retirement plans to generate additional government revenue. One such example is House Resolution (HR) 4348, "The Moving Ahead for Progress in the 21st Century Act (MAP-21)," which became law on July 6, 2012. This bill was primarily intended to fund the nation's infrastructure surrounding transportation programs, but it included pension plan changes that allowed the government to raise funds for the infrastructure bill itself.

The government cannot make money other than through taxes, so they reallocated funds to collect more taxes. In a 401(K) retirement plan, the participant and employer make contributions that will not be taxed for 30 years, meaning the government will not receive revenue from that income placed in the retirement plan. To provide funding for MAP-21, Congress made provisions allowing employers to pay less into retirement plans instead of providing a complete match bonus, which would raise $9.4 billion over ten years. This means that $9.4 billion was redirected from America's retirement plans to fund America's infrastructure.

If the expected 8 percent growth is compounded over 30 years, the government hijacked the potential of $94 billion from American citizens' retirement plans. The MAP-21 provision also increased premiums paid by employers from $35 per participant to $49, which would raise $11.2 billion over ten years for the government. The bill included other provisions on pension plan transfer that would also benefit the government, allowing them to raise an additional $354 million. This one piece of legislation raised $20.9 billion from the revision of 401(K) pension plans to pay for the MAP-21 Infrastructure bill, which had the potential growth of $210.8 billion if kept in the 401(K) plans.

In 2012, the US government redirected funds from retirement plans, depriving millions of Americans of the opportunity to retire with enough money in their plans. This legislation is merely an illustration of how bills may seem to be beneficial, but they can result in taking away funds. In 2021, Congress looked for more ways to fund the new $3.5 trillion Reconciliation stimulus bill, and due to the disagreement on lifting the debt ceiling, they looked again at pension plans to do so. Over 65 proposals were sent to revise and reconcile pension plans to raise funds for the $3.5 trillion reconciliation bill.

To take control of your financial future, creating a banking system that you can manage independently is crucial, particularly given the impact of legislative decisions and other factors outside your control. This involves leveraging tools such as real estate, max-funded life insurance policies, infinite banking policies, and decentralized finance. With the advent of blockchain technology, it is now possible to take complete control of your finances without the intervention of traditional financial institutions. In upcoming chapters, we will explore leveraging cryptocurrency and decentralized finance to create your banking system through the blockchain. Since the US dollar has not been backed by gold since 1971, it has become a fiat currency that is subject to the unlimited printing of money by the Federal Reserve, which slowly devalues the buying power of the dollar. This system is slowly eroding the wealth of those who work for and save the dollar. However, new-age digital assets that increase in value, free from manipulation by Wall Street, offer an opportunity to back your dollar and create a more secure financial future. We can show you how to make money off your debt and spending, so continue reading and let's get you unbanked!

Chapter Six: Creating Your Banking System

"Banking establishments are more dangerous than standing armies."

– Thomas Jefferson

Creating your banking system may sound daunting, but it is a valuable and beneficial opportunity for families and the next generation. By leveraging cryptocurrency, money markets, real estate, and a max-funded life insurance policy, individuals can take control of their financial future and establish a secure and stable financial foundation for their families.

One of the key benefits of creating your banking system is having complete control over your finances. Traditional banking systems rely on centralized institutions to manage transactions, investments, and loans. However, these institutions are subject to government regulations, market fluctuations, and internal corruption. This can lead to decreased trust in the system and even financial losses for individuals. By leveraging cryptocurrency and other alternative investment options, individuals can reduce reliance on traditional banking systems and establish a more secure and stable financial foundation.

    Cryptocurrency, in particular, offers several benefits over traditional banking systems. One of cryptocurrency's primary advantages is its level of security. Cryptocurrencies like Bitcoin and Ethereum use advanced cryptographic algorithms to secure transactions and prevent fraud. Cryptocurrencies are decentralized, meaning they are not controlled by any central authority or government. This makes them immune to the same market fluctuations and government regulations that traditional banking systems are subject to.

    Another benefit of creating your banking system is generating passive income through investments in real estate and money markets. Real estate investments can provide long-term growth and stability, while money market investments offer high liquidity and low risk. Additionally, investments in a max-funded life insurance policy can provide tax-free growth and the ability to borrow against the policy's cash value. Creating your banking system can also provide financial security for the next generation. Individuals can ensure their family's financial well-being for years by establishing a secure and stable financial foundation. This can include setting up trust funds, establishing a financial education plan for children, and investing in long-term growth opportunities that can provide a legacy of financial stability.

It is important to note that creating your banking system requires careful planning, research, and guidance from financial professionals. While the benefits are numerous, there are risks associated with alternative investment options and cryptocurrencies. It is crucial to work with a trusted financial advisor who can help guide you through the process and ensure that your investments are aligned with your financial goals and risk tolerance.

In addition to building your banking system, it is essential to have a comprehensive understanding of how to accumulate wealth. We have outlined several steps that you can apply in your life to achieve this goal. The first and most critical step in this process is becoming aware of your current financial situation by determining your net worth, which is calculated by subtracting your total debts from your total assets. The next step is to create a plan to save at least 10 to 20 percent of your income each month. If you do not have extra income, you may need to consider getting a side gig to have money to save and invest. After accumulating money, you will need to explore various financial vehicles to find the best option for building wealth. We will discuss some of these vehicles in the upcoming chapters.

Lastly, to optimally accumulate wealth, it is essential to get lean with your finances and invest in your future. Here are a few straightforward rules to follow: spend and live on less than you earn, invest at least 10-30 percent of your monthly income, resist the temptation to put all of your eggs in one basket, and ensure that you have a basic understanding of the fees and costs associated with the financial vehicles you plan to leverage to build wealth.

In conclusion, creating your banking system using cryptocurrency, brokerage accounts, real estate, and a max-funded life insurance policy can provide individuals and families with complete control over their finances, increased security, and the ability to generate passive income. It presents an opportunity to establish a secure and stable financial foundation for your family and future generations. Although alternative investment options and cryptocurrencies have risks, the benefits are numerous and can lead to financial independence and stability. Collaborating with a trusted financial advisor ensures that your investments align with your objectives and risk tolerance.

Chapter Seven: The Blockchain and Cryptocurrency Explained

"Bitcoin is digital gold growing harder, smarter, faster, and stronger due to the relentless progression of technology."

– Michael J. Saylor

On January 3rd, 2009, the Bitcoin network was launched when an individual or group known as Satoshi Nakamoto mined the first bitcoin block, block zero, which rewarded them with 50 bitcoins. Although the exact reason for launching this new peer-to-peer currency system remains unknown, it was a timely arrival for a world needing financial alternatives to the outdated central banking system. Perhaps it was due to the banks' continuous gross misuse of the monetary system, the constant printing of money, the 2007-2009 recession, or the $700 billion bailout of the banking system that led to the US economy's state at the time. Despite the motive, Satoshi Nakamoto provided the world with another option to avoid succumbing to the banking system's continuous failure. In October 2008, we were forced to witness the government approve the Troubled Asset Relief Program (TARP), which involved bailing out the banks by purchasing all the toxic assets they had risked. The situation worsened as bank executives received bonuses totaling $1.6 billion despite having caused the system's collapse. People needed independence and control over their money, away from this broken banking system. So, what exactly is Blockchain Technology, and how does it work?

Blockchain Technology Explained

Blockchain is a digital ledger that stores information in a decentralized manner, unlike the centralized mechanisms used by the banking system in the past. Decentralized refers to a distributed ledger requiring a computer or user network to validate transactions that enter and get locked onto the blockchain ledger after validation. This technology eliminates the need for a central authority, which removes the potential for bad actors to manipulate the system. Let's compare this to the ledger banks currently use as a central authority system.

When you visit a bank to make a deposit, the teller first asks for your account number, then verifies your identity to ensure you are the account owner. Once verified, they allow you to withdraw or deposit money onto their ledger. For example, if you were making a deposit, you'd give the teller $1,000, and the teller would then log it onto the bank's ledger under your account number. Only the bank and its authorized employees can view the bank ledger. Although the current banking system may seem promising based on central control and complete trust in third parties, these central ledgers' countless thefts and manipulations have proven dangerous for bank customers. An internet search of bank tellers across the globe who became bad actors in the system reveals numerous thefts and hacks of these bank ledgers by their very own employees. The gatekeepers of the centralized ledgers were able to manipulate this system to steal money, and sometimes it went unnoticed by the customer.

    For banks to have a genuinely secure ledger, they would need multiple people who don't have the same interests or don't know each other to validate transactions before they get added. This would be a prolonged and costly process, requiring six people to review a customer transaction before a deposit or withdrawal could happen. This is where Blockchain Technology provides a solution. Data is entered on the blockchain through the authentication of each user's cryptographic keys to identify their wallet or account. After the user is identified, their request goes through a process before being added to the blockchain. In the figure below, the first step starts with a transaction request that must be authenticated. Once authenticated, a block is created for that transaction and then sent to every node in the network for validation.

On bitcoin.org, they explain how to participate in the peer-to-peer system as a node. A node is a program that runs on a computer that validates transactions and blockchain blocks. Once the transaction is validated by the nodes, they receive a reward in the form of cryptocurrency, and the block gets added to the existing blockchain. Then, the update gets sent across the entire system. This makes it impossible for bad players to manipulate the system as they would have to know every node (participant) validating transactions to defraud the system.

How Are Transactions added onto the Blockchain

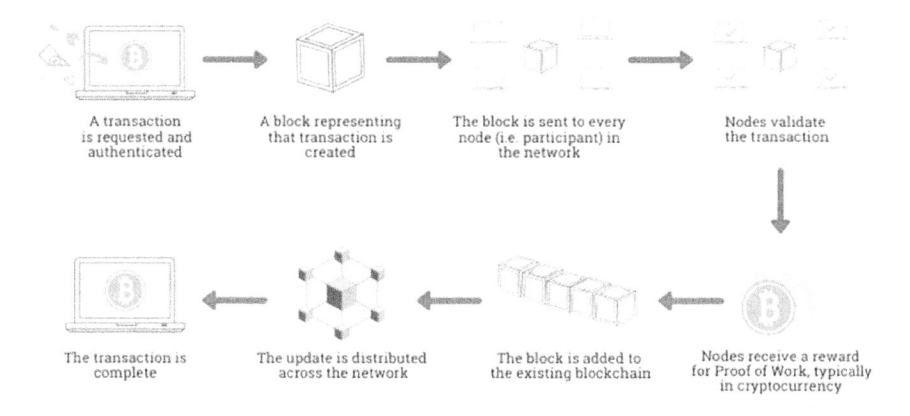

A transaction is requested and authenticated	
A block representing that transaction is created	
The block is sent to every node (i.e. participant) in the network	
Nodes validate the transaction	
Nodes receive a reward for Proof of Work, typically in cryptocurrency	
The block is added to the existing blockchain	
The update is distributed across the network	
The transaction is complete	

The Blockchain is a 24/7 system, enabling payments to be sent anytime and anywhere globally at a fraction of the cost. Traditional banking systems require forms to be filled out and a $40-70 payment sent to the bank for wiring money. Such transactions usually take 3-7 business days and can only be initiated between 8 am to 5 pm, Monday through Friday. In contrast, the same transaction can be completed in minutes at a significantly lower cost on the blockchain. Additionally, as an open-source code, the blockchain is fully transparent, allowing anyone to view the code. Bitcoin transaction requests validated on the platform are visible to the public on websites like blockchain.com, providing additional transparency. Now that we have a basic understanding of blockchain technology let's dive into how it powers the most well-known cryptocurrency, Bitcoin.

Bitcoin Explained

Bitcoin is a digital currency that operates through a peer-to-peer system, allowing for direct transactions between individuals without financial institutions acting as intermediaries. Unlike traditional payment systems that rely on trusted third parties like banks to process electronic payments, bitcoin utilizes cryptography to secure and validate transactions on a decentralized network known as the blockchain. By eliminating the need for bank tellers and other intermediaries in the payment process, bitcoin transactions can be conducted faster, cheaper, and with greater security. This has made it possible for individuals worldwide to send and receive currency at any time, from anywhere, without having to pay the high fees associated with traditional banking systems. While bitcoin is still a relatively new concept, it has already proven to be a powerful tool for those looking to take greater control over their finances and bypass the limitations of traditional payment systems.

Cryptocurrency Security

Cryptocurrency security is one of the most significant benefits of blockchain technology. Each transaction is secured by an immutable cryptographic signature called a hash, which is added to the blockchain ledger. The use of cryptography makes it virtually impossible to alter any transaction on the blockchain without being detected. Additionally, blockchains are designed to be highly resistant to tampering or hacking. As mentioned previously, each block in the chain contains a hash linked to the previous block, creating a chain of blocks that can be traced back to the first block in the chain, known as the genesis block. The distributed nature of the blockchain means that every participant on the network has a copy of the entire ledger, which makes it highly resistant to attacks. Furthermore, to make changes to the blockchain, a consensus must be reached among the participants on the network. This means that a majority of the network must agree upon any proposed changes, making it nearly impossible for a single party to make unauthorized changes. While no system is entirely foolproof, blockchain technology in cryptocurrencies has proven to be a highly secure and reliable method for conducting transactions without needing a trusted intermediary.

Blockchain technology has revolutionized the way we think about financial transactions, allowing for a decentralized system that eliminates the need for trust in centralized institutions like banks. As a peer-to-peer digital currency built on the blockchain, Bitcoin provides an alternative option to the traditional banking system, allowing for fast, secure, and cost-effective transactions worldwide. With the added layer of cryptographic security, the blockchain provides an immutable and transparent record of all transactions that cannot be tampered with, adding to the overall security of the ledger. As the world evolves and technology advances, it will be interesting to see how blockchain and cryptocurrency continue to disrupt and transform the financial landscape.

In upcoming chapters, we will review tools that can be leveraged in a banking system, like real estate, max-funded life insurance policies, infinite banking policies, and decentralized finance.

Chapter Eight: The Power of Decentralized Finance (DeFi)

"In decentralized finance, we are not only democratizing access to financial tools, but also empowering individuals to control their own financial destiny."

– Stani Kulechov

Decentralized Finance (DeFi) is a technology that offers an alternative approach to building a banking system, free from the constraints of traditional banking institutions. DeFi operates on a blockchain, which is a decentralized and immutable ledger that records all transactions. Unlike traditional banking, DeFi is open to everyone and can be accessed anywhere worldwide without restrictions or limitations. With DeFi, you have complete control over your finances and are your own bank.

One of the most significant advantages of DeFi is the ability to earn passive income. There are several ways to earn passive income with DeFi, such as lending, staking, and yield farming. Lending allows you to earn interest on your crypto assets by lending them to other users on the platform. Staking involves holding a certain amount of a particular cryptocurrency and earning rewards for validating transactions on the blockchain. Yield farming uses various DeFi protocols to optimize returns and earn the highest yield.

Another advantage of DeFi is the ability to trade assets without intermediaries. Decentralized exchanges (DEXs) allow you to trade cryptocurrencies peer-to-peer without needing a centralized exchange or a middleman. This means you have complete control over your assets and can trade them anytime without restrictions or fees.

To set up a banking system with DeFi, you first need to create a digital wallet that will allow you to store and manage your cryptocurrency assets. Several wallets, both hardware, and software, offer various levels of security and accessibility. Once you have a wallet, you can deposit your crypto assets into DeFi protocols and earn passive income.

When choosing a DeFi protocol, it is essential to research and selects a secure and reliable platform. Look for protocols that have been audited by reputable firms and have a good track record of performance. It is also essential to consider the fees associated with DeFi protocols, as some platforms charge higher fees than others.

In summary, DeFi provides a new way of creating a banking system free from traditional institutions. With DeFi, you have complete control over your finances, and you can earn passive income by lending, staking, and yield farming. Decentralized exchanges allow you to trade cryptocurrencies peer-to-peer without intermediaries, giving you full control over your assets. To set up a banking system with DeFi, you need to create a digital wallet and deposit your assets into secure and reliable DeFi protocols. By leveraging the power of DeFi, you can take control of your finances and create a banking system that works for you.

Chapter Nine: Creating a Personal Banking System with Max-Funded and Infinite Banking Policies

"Life insurance is not for the people who die; it's for the people who live."

– Dave Ramsey

When creating a personal banking system, one of the most effective tools individuals can use is a life insurance policy. Specifically, max-funded life insurance and infinite banking policies have proven to be highly effective in creating a personal banking system that offers numerous benefits.

Max-funded life insurance policies, also known as high cash-value life insurance policies, are a form of permanent life insurance. They are designed to build up a significant cash value over time, which the policyholder can then access tax-free. These policies are unique in allowing policyholders to overfund the policy, which means they can contribute more than the required premium payments. Doing so allows the policyholder to accumulate cash value faster than a traditional life insurance policy.

In addition to providing a death benefit to beneficiaries, max-funded life insurance policies can be used as a personal banking system. The policyholder can access the policy's cash value at any time, tax-free. This means that the cash value can be used to pay for expenses, such as college tuition, a down payment on a house, or even as a source of income in retirement. Essentially, a max-funded life insurance policy acts as a savings account that grows tax-free.

Infinite banking policies are another type of life insurance policy that can be used to create a personal banking system. Infinite banking was a concept developed by Nelson Nash, who believed that individuals should become their bankers. The idea behind infinite banking is to use a dividend-paying whole life insurance policy as a savings vehicle. By overfunding the policy, policyholders can build up a significant cash value that can be used as a source of funding for loans.

Infinite banking policies work by allowing policyholders to take out loans against the policy's cash value. The policyholder pays interest on the loan, but the interest is paid back to the policyholder, which means that the policyholder is essentially borrowing money from themselves. This concept is based on the idea that the policyholder can recapture the interest paid to a traditional bank. In addition to providing a source of funding for loans, infinite banking policies offer numerous other benefits. For example, the policy's cash value grows at a tax-free rate, and the death benefit is paid out tax-free to beneficiaries. This means that infinite banking policies can be used as a tool for estate planning.

To create a personal banking system with max-funded and infinite banking policies, working with a knowledgeable financial advisor in these areas is vital. A financial professional can help individuals determine the correct policy type for their specific needs and guide how to structure the policy to maximize its benefits. When creating a personal banking system with life insurance policies, it is essential to remember that these policies are not a substitute for traditional savings and investment vehicles. While they can provide numerous benefits, they should be used with other tools and strategies to create a comprehensive financial plan.

Max-funded life insurance and infinite banking policies offer individuals a unique and effective way to create a personal banking system. By overfunding these policies, individuals can build up a significant cash value that can be accessed tax-free and used as a source of funding for loans or as a savings account that grows at a tax-free rate. However, working with a financial professional knowledgeable in these areas is essential to ensure that the policy is structured correctly and maximizes its benefits.

Chapter Ten: Creating a Banking System with Your Brokerage Account

"The way to make money is to buy when blood is running in the streets."

– John D. Rockefeller

A brokerage account is a type of investment account that allows you to buy and sell stocks, bonds, mutual funds, and other securities. The process of setting up a brokerage account is straightforward. You can open one with a brokerage firm, either online or in person. One of the main benefits of a brokerage account is the ability to invest in a wide range of financial instruments. This means that you can diversify your portfolio and earn higher returns. Additionally, brokerage accounts offer tax benefits such as tax-deferred or tax-free growth, depending on your account type.

There are two main brokerage account types: cash and margin. A cash account allows you to invest using only the funds you deposited into the account. On the other hand, a margin account allows you to borrow money from the brokerage firm to invest. While brokerage accounts offer many advantages, they also come with some risks. The stock market is unpredictable and can fluctuate, so there is always a risk of losing money. Additionally, fees and commissions can eat into your investment returns, so it is essential to research and choose a brokerage firm that offers competitive rates.

When choosing a brokerage firm, there are a few things to consider. First, look for a firm with a good reputation and track record. You can read reviews online and ask for recommendations from friends and family. Additionally, consider the fees and commissions that the firm charges and the types of investment products they offer. Once you have chosen a brokerage firm, opening an account is simple. You must provide personal information such as your name, address, and social security number. You will also need to fund your account by depositing money into it.

Once your account is set up, you can invest in various financial instruments. You can invest in individual stocks, bonds, mutual funds, etc. Do your research and choose investments that align with your financial goals and risk tolerance. A brokerage account can be a valuable tool in creating your banking system. It offers many investment options and tax benefits but comes with some risks. By choosing a reputable brokerage firm and investing wisely, you can earn higher returns and take control of your financial future.

The information provided in this chapter is for educational purposes only and should not be taken as financial advice. It is important to consult a licensed financial advisor before making financial decisions. Using brokerage accounts as a banking system has risks, and it is crucial to understand those risks before investing. It is recommended to seek professional financial advice before opening a brokerage account or investing in the stock market. A financial advisor can provide personalized guidance based on your financial goals and risk tolerance. They can also help you develop a diversified investment portfolio that aligns with your long-term financial objectives.

Chapter Eleven: Leveraging Real Estate in a Banking System

"Real estate cannot be lost or stolen, nor can it be carried away. Purchased with common sense, paid for in full, and managed with reasonable care, it is about the safest investment in the world."

– Franklin D. Roosevelt

Real estate is a tangible asset that can be leveraged as a banking system in multiple ways. By using the equity in your real estate, you can access funds to invest, start a business, or improve your financial situation. This paper will explore how real estate can be used as a banking system and each method's potential benefits and drawbacks.

One way to use real estate as a banking system is through a home equity loan or line of credit. This involves borrowing against the equity in your home, which is the difference between the home's value and any outstanding mortgage balance. Home equity loans typically have fixed interest rates. They are paid back in regular installments over a set period, while home equity lines of credit work more like credit cards, with a variable interest rate and a maximum credit limit that can be drawn upon as needed.

Another way to leverage real estate as a banking system is through a cash-out refinance. This involves refinancing your mortgage for more than you currently owe and taking the difference in cash. The new mortgage usually has a higher interest rate than your original mortgage, but it can be a way to access a significant amount of funds in one lump sum.

Real estate can also be used as a banking system through investment properties. By purchasing a rental property, you can generate income through rental payments and appreciate the property's value over time. This income and equity can be used to fund other investments or expenses. Another option for using real estate as a banking system is a sale-leaseback arrangement. This involves selling your property to an investor and then leasing it back. This can provide immediate cash flow while allowing you to live or work on the property. However, it also means giving up property ownership and potentially paying higher rent in the long run.

One potential drawback of using real estate as a banking system is the risk involved. Property values or rental income decreases could impact your ability to repay loans or mortgages. Additionally, if you use your home as collateral, there is always the risk of foreclosure if you cannot make payments. Considering the costs of using real estate as a banking system is essential. Fees for home equity loans or cash-out refinances can be high, and additional expenses may be associated with maintaining an investment property or selling and leasing back a property. Despite these potential drawbacks, real estate can be a valuable tool for creating a personal banking system. By leveraging the equity in your property or generating income through rental properties, you can access funds to achieve your financial goals.

It is crucial to seek advice from a qualified real estate professional before utilizing real estate as a banking system. Such guidance can assist in identifying the optimal options for an individual's financial situation and provide insight into navigating the potential risks and costs associated with this approach. Careful consideration and prudent decision-making are essential when leveraging real estate.

Bonus Chapter Twelve: How to Purchase Your First Real Estate Asset with 0-3.5% Down

"Real estate cannot be lost or stolen, nor can it be carried away. Purchased with common sense, paid for in full, and managed with reasonable care, it is about the safest investment in the world."
– Franklin D. Roosevelt

This chapter will discuss purchasing a 1–4-unit property with VA and FHA loans. These loans require only a 0-3.5 percent down payment, making it easier for potential homeowners to finance their purchases.

A VA loan is a mortgage loan offered by the United States Department of Veterans Affairs to help veterans, active-duty service members, and their eligible spouses purchase a home. With a VA loan, you can buy a 1–4-unit property without any down payment. This means you can purchase a property with no money out of your pocket, making it an attractive option for those with limited funds for a down payment. The eligibility criteria for a VA loan include serving in the military or being a surviving spouse of a veteran who died while on duty or due to a service-related disability. The

VA loan also requires a particular credit score, debt-to-income ratio, and proof of income.

On the other hand, an FHA loan is a mortgage loan insured by the Federal Housing Administration, a government agency within the U.S. Department of Housing and Urban Development. An FHA loan requires a down payment of only 3.5 percent, significantly lower than most lenders' traditional 20 percent down payment. FHA loans are available to anyone who meets the eligibility requirements, including first-time homebuyers and individuals with a low credit scores. However, there are limits on the amount you can borrow with an FHA loan, and you will also need to pay for mortgage insurance, which protects the lender in case of default.

When purchasing a 1–4-unit property with either a VA or FHA loan, it is vital to understand the advantages and disadvantages of each loan option. VA loans offer the advantage of no down payment, while FHA loans require a lower down payment than traditional loans. However, both loans have eligibility requirements that must be met, and additional costs such as mortgage insurance and funding fees may apply. You can work with a mortgage lender or broker to apply for a VA or FHA loan. A mortgage lender is a financial institution that provides mortgage loans directly to borrowers. In contrast, a mortgage broker acts as a middleman between the borrower and the lender, helping to find the best loan options and rates.

Before applying for a loan, gathering the necessary documents, such as income statements, tax returns, and credit reports, is essential. Getting pre-approved for a loan is also recommended, which can give you a better idea of how much you can afford to borrow and help you make a more informed decision when purchasing a property. Purchasing a 1–4-unit property with a VA or FHA loan can be an excellent option for those with limited funds for a down payment. While each loan option has its advantages and disadvantages, it is essential to consult with a mortgage lender or broker to determine the best option for your financial situation.

After discussing some financing options for securing your property with minimal down payment, the next step is to find a property that you can live in and generate cash flow. It is worth noting that, as long as the property has four units or less, it is considered a residual property and not commercial. My first 4-plex was purchased using a VA loan, which allowed me to walk into a real estate deal with zero capital down. Moreover, I learned how to enter the deal with profit at the table as well.

When I initially bought the 4-unit complex, it was 100% occupied with two tenants paying $1,500 a month and the other two paying $1,000 a month, bringing the total monthly rental income to $5,000. This meant that once I owned the property, I would be collecting $5,000 a month in rental income, which is a good profit situation to start with. I was able to collect $5,000 in profit at closing by strategically closing the deal at the right time. Therefore, you should learn this wealth concept to walk into a profitable deal as well.

Mortgage terms can vary depending on the lender's policies and agreement, so it is essential to do your due diligence when selecting a lender. However, most lenders operate in the following way: when you close on a mortgage loan, your first payment is typically not due until the first day of the month following the month in which you closed your mortgage. For instance, when I closed on my 4-plex, I chose to close on the 2nd of March, which meant that my first payment to the bank would be due on May 1st. This allowed me to collect two months' rent before making my first payment to the bank, a strategy that can be used for any investment property.

It is crucial to choose a real estate agent who understands your investment goals. In my situation, I walked away with $5,000 at the table, and the next month I collected another $5,000, resulting in a profit of $10,000 for a property that we put zero money down on. If you are both the real estate agent and the buyer, the deal gets even sweeter because you not only collect rent as the property owner but also earn a 3 percent commission on the deal. In my real-life scenario, I was also the agent and was able to walk away with an additional $4,000 in commission. Therefore, before any payment was made to the bank, we produced a total profit of $14,000 just by buying the property. This is a wealth concept worth keeping in your toolbox. It is important to mention that when using an FHA or VA loan, you must occupy the property, so clarify the amount of time you must physically live in the residence with your lender.

In summary, purchasing a 1-4 unit property with VA and FHA loans can be an excellent option for potential homeowners with limited funds for a down payment. While VA loans require no down payment, FHA loans require a lower down payment than traditional loans. It's essential to understand the eligibility requirements and additional costs associated with each loan option before making a decision. Working with a mortgage lender or broker can help you find the best loan options and rates. Additionally, it's crucial to gather the necessary documents and get pre-approved for a loan before making a purchase. Furthermore, purchasing a 1-4 unit property can be a profitable investment, especially when using strategies such as buying residual properties with zero capital down and closing the deal at the right time. Choosing a real estate agent who understands your investment goals can help you maximize your profits, and when using an FHA or VA loan, clarify the amount of time you must physically live in the residence with your lender. In summary, this chapter has provided valuable insights into financing options for securing a property and generating cash flow, setting the stage for the book's conclusion, which will explore additional wealth-building concepts in real estate.

Conclusion

"A truly open and decentralized financial system has the potential to empower individuals, promote transparency, and level the playing field for all, ultimately creating a more inclusive and free world."

– Unknown

In today's volatile economic climate, a personal banking system can provide individuals and families with greater financial security and control. This strategy involves leveraging a variety of financial instruments, including real estate, insurance policies, cryptocurrency, money market accounts, and brokerage accounts, to create a diversified portfolio that provides income and growth potential. Additionally, integrating cryptocurrency and Decentralized Finance (DeFi) into the banking industry has expanded the options for creating a personal banking system.

A real estate asset is a powerful tool for creating a personal banking system. Using real estate as collateral, individuals can access funds through home equity lines of credit or by refinancing their mortgage. Additionally, investing in rental properties can provide individuals with passive income streams that can help supplement their other income sources. While risks are associated with investing in real estate, the potential rewards can be significant.

Insurance policies, including max-funded life insurance and infinite banking policies, can also be used as part of a personal banking system. By utilizing the cash value of these policies, individuals can access funds to supplement their income or make investments. Additionally, these policies offer tax benefits and provide individuals with financial security that other investment vehicles may not offer.

Money market accounts provide individuals with a safe and low-risk option for creating a personal banking system. While the returns on these accounts are relatively low, they offer stability and liquidity that can be invaluable in economic uncertainty. Money market accounts can also fund short-term goals like vacations or home renovations. Brokerage accounts are another option for individuals looking to create a personal banking system. By investing in stocks, bonds, and other securities, individuals can earn higher returns than they would with traditional savings accounts. However, investing in the stock market comes with inherent risks, and individuals should carefully consider their risk tolerance and investment goals before investing.

Integrating cryptocurrency into the banking industry can improve the speed, security, and efficiency of financial transactions. Cryptocurrency can provide a decentralized and secure payment system that is not reliant on traditional financial institutions. Transactions can be completed instantly and with low transaction fees, making it an attractive alternative to traditional banking systems. Additionally, cryptocurrency is highly transparent, and its decentralized nature can help to prevent fraud and money laundering. Cryptocurrency can also provide greater financial privacy for individuals, as transactions can be made anonymously. Furthermore, DeFi allows individuals to earn interest on their cryptocurrency holdings, providing passive income without relying on traditional banking institutions.

By combining these financial instruments, individuals can create a diversified portfolio that provides income and growth potential. Individuals can attain financial freedom and lead a more comfortable lifestyle by depending on the interest generated from their investments rather than traditional income sources. This is especially important in today's economic climate, with high uncertainty and volatility. Individuals can protect themselves against economic downturns and other financial risks by diversifying their portfolios and creating multiple income streams.

Creating a personal banking system also offers individuals greater autonomy over their finances. Additionally, a personal banking system can assist individuals in reaching long-term financial objectives, including saving for retirement, financing their children's education, or acquiring a home, with increased efficiency and effectiveness.

Despite the many advantages of creating a personal banking system, it is crucial to recognize that this strategy requires careful planning and execution. Individuals should work with financial advisors and other professionals to develop a strategy that aligns with their long-term financial goals and risk tolerance. Individuals should regularly review and adjust their strategy to account for changes in their financial situation or the broader economic landscape.

In conclusion, creating a personal banking system using a combination of real estate, insurance policies, cryptocurrency, money market accounts, and brokerage accounts can provide individuals and families with greater financial security and flexibility. Remember that individual options expand by integrating cryptocurrency and DeFi into the banking industry. With careful planning and execution, individuals can achieve financial independence and live a comfortable lifestyle by creating a diversified portfolio of financial instruments.

Acknowledgements

I would like to express my heartfelt gratitude to the love of my life, my wife, and business partner, Wanda Webb, for her unwavering patience and belief in my abilities throughout the process of completing this book. From the countless late nights and coffee shop visits to the early mornings, Wanda was always prepared for anything that needed to be done. Her daily words of affirmation and steadfast support kept me focused and motivated to see this project through to the end.

There were times when Wanda believed in my abilities more than I did myself, and her unwavering faith in me has made all the difference. As we reflect on our incredible 15-year journey together, I am immensely grateful that we have been able to compile and share some of our most valuable lessons in this book.

This book would not have been possible without Wanda's constant encouragement, love, and support. To her, I offer my deepest thanks and appreciation for being my rock and my inspiration throughout this journey. It is my sincere hope that our experiences and insights will be of value to our readers, just as they have been to us.

Notes

Meet The Author

Randy Webb, Jr. is a retired Air Force pilot, entrepreneur, real estate investor, business consultant, author, speaker, and financial educator. He currently resides in Dallas, Texas with his wife Wanda and five children. He holds a Bachelors of Science degree in Professional Aeronautics from Embry-Riddle Aeronautical University and a Masters of Science degree in Human Resource Management from Troy University. Randy's unwavering commitment to education has led him to pursue a Doctorate of Business Administration at Walden University, further expanding his knowledge and expertise. Randy is a natural problem solver with a passion for executing tasks and solving problems in a timely manner. In addition to his military background, Randy is a licensed insurance broker who specializes in helping others accumulate wealth through various life insurance vehicles. Furthermore, Randy has a passion for real estate investing, trading, and teaching on mindset and money. As an author, speaker, and financial educator, Randy is dedicated to helping others achieve financial independence through sound investment strategies and a positive mindset. His commitment to helping others succeed is unmatched, and he is known for his ability to inspire and motivate others to achieve their financial goals.

Made in the USA
Las Vegas, NV
05 May 2023